WRITE

UP

FRONT

Cynthia K. Erbes
S.J. Di Christina
Erie Community College
North Campus
Buffalo, NY

KENDALL/HUNT PUBLISHING COMPANY
4050 Westmark Drive   Dubuque, Iowa 52002

Cover design by Marcia M. Holler

TABLE OF CONTENTS

SECTION THREE: GRAMMAR

Preface

This text is uniquely designed for those colleges that offer two developmental/remedial levels of English prior to a degree credit composition course. At Erie Community College, for example, we offer a first level developmental English course for those students whose writing skills are severely limited; i.e., inability to write complete sentences, to develop paragraph structure, to express ideas clearly and coherently. The second level of developmental English is for those students whose writing skills are moderately limited; i.e., inability to coordinate and subordinate ideas, to develop ideas fully, to organize ideas logically and fluidly. We have found that some highly motivated students in first level developmental English, however, are able to grasp both levels within one semester, thereby skipping the second level.

Our purposes in designing this text are twofold: to aid those highly motivated students and to reach the diverse population of developmental courses that may include ESL students, handicapped students, nontraditional students as well as recent high school graduates. Students are encouraged to proceed at their own pace in mastering the skills necessary to become better writers. The text is constructed so that each student may begin writing immediately — or *right up front*.

Write Up Front contains several distinctive features:

⇒ **Two levels of exercises for each chapter of the text.** The first level contains relatively simple exercises while the second level contains more challenging and longer exercises.

⇒ **Relevant exercises.** Exercises concern the "real" world and provide information as well as aid in mastering specific skills.

⇒ **Immediate writing assignments.** The student is encouraged to begin writing as soon as possible and may progress at his or her own pace.

⇒ **Student generated examples.** By providing work completed by actual developmental students, we can encourage current students.

⇒ **Three independent sections.** The first section concerns the initial steps in the writing process; the second section concerns the content and organization of both paragraphs and essays while the third section concentrates on grammatical skills. This allows the instructor to begin with any of the three sections or to use any sections concurrently.

⇒ **Humor.** Throughout the text, the predominant attitude toward writing is that writing can be an exciting adventure of both self-discovery and communication in order to motivate those students whose insecurity with or hostility toward English hampers their mastery of the writing skills necessary to survive their academic life and their future employment.

⇒ **Introductions highlighting key chapter points.** Each chapter begins with an overview of the chapter's contents for quick reference.

For developmental students, these features help motivate them in their mastery of English writing skills, provide encouragement to progress at a comfortable rate, and make learning the skills they need easy and painless. For developmental instructors, these features make the text flexible in its application so that each instructor can modify its use for his or her own particular classes. The text will work as both a focal point for individual achievement and for group activity. It may also be used as a reference text in both developmental courses and in college composition courses.

Section one — PLANNING THE PARAGRAPH OR ESSAY — contains two chapters: Prewriting and Organizing Ideas. These chapters help the student find ideas, develop ideas and organize ideas culminating in the basic essay. Section two — WRITING THE PARAGRAPHS — contains four chapters: The Body Paragraph, Introductions, Conclusion, and Putting the Essay Together. These chapters aid the student in mastering the basic thesis and support essay. Section three — GRAMMAR — consists of nine chapters: Parts of Speech, Coordination, Subordination, Run-ons and Comma Splices, Fragments, Pronouns and Agreement, Subject-Verb Agreement, Basic Punctuation, and Glossary of Confusing Words. These chapters explain the rudiments of basic sentence structure and coherence.

Write Up Front empowers students with the ability to communicate clearly and succinctly by making the writing process both pleasurable and relevant and assists instructors in creating a flexible learning environment.

We gratefully acknowledge Marcia Holler, Graphics Editor of *ELF: Eclectic Literary Forum*; Suzanne Neubauer, Publisher of *ELF: Eclectic Literary Forum*; and John K. Park. Their assistance in design, production and proofreading has been invaluable. We also thank all of our students, particularly John Boeckel and Edward P. Kruger, for their help in providing material and support for our efforts.

Chapter One

Prewriting

1.1 Choosing a Topic

Mental Encyclopedia
Freewriting

1.2 Developing Ideas

Focused Freewriting
Listing
Brainstorming
Clustering

KEY TERMS

Brainstorming .... asking questions to develop ideas

Clustering .... using circles to arrange ideas

Focused Freewriting .... writing on a specific subject
without regard to grammar

Freewriting .... writing without regard to grammar

Listing .... listing all ideas about a topic

Mental Encyclopedia .... mental catalogue of ideas

Prewriting .... all writing done before the rough draft

Suppose someone gave you a truckload of lumber, a pail of nails, and a hammer, and then told you to build a house. After the shock wore off, you might not have any idea where to begin. Much the same is true if a teacher tells you to take out a sheet of paper and write an essay. Beginning is always the difficult part. It's even more difficult if you have no plan.

As you need a plan to build a house, so you need a plan to make a paragraph or essay, a blueprint you can follow. The first step in the writing process helps you make that plan.

Prewriting is making a plan to write a paragraph or an essay. It is all the preparation you do before you ever start to write your paragraph or essay. This step is one of the most important. Poor planning can lead you to creating an odd shack of a paragraph or essay. A well-thought out blueprint makes your essay or paragraph a beautiful sight; it also helps you write that paragraph or essay faster with far less perspiration.

1.1 Choosing A Topic

Choosing a topic is the first order of business. Where will this topic come from? Unless you're specifically given a topic and told to read about it in encyclopedias, books and magazines, the topic must come from what you know.

❏ **Mental Encyclopedia**

You carry with you a *mental encyclopedia* full of information. All you have to do is tap into that knowledge. To make it easier for you to sort through this mental encyclopedia, think of all the information in your mind as divided into categories such as these:

Mental Encyclopedia	Acquaintances Hobbies Children Movies College Music Education Social Issues Experiences Sports Family Television Friends Vacations Games Values

As you sift through the categories, and perhaps add a few of your own, consider the topic that appeals to you the most, the one about which you are most passionate. It's always easier to write about topics you enjoy and know something about.

The reader, usually the instructor, is a stranger to you — a reader you are trying to reach. The more interesting the information, the more likely the reader will enjoy your writing.

❑ Freewriting

Freewriting is another way of finding a topic you might like to write about. Freewriting is exactly what it sounds like — it's "free" of all the restrictions that come with writing for a reader. The only one who's going to read your freewriting is *you*! You don't need to worry about misspellings, sentences, or paragraphing.

You write whatever comes into your head, however it pops out of your pen. However, there is one catch — you need to set a time limit, perhaps five to ten minutes. This isn't speed writing, so you don't have to write until your hand cramps. Just write as much as you can in the time limit. The following is an example:

Freewriting Sample

(1) I dont know why I'm sitting here writing this stupid thing that no ones going to read Id rather be on the beach in Florida sitting in the sand away from all this snow. (2) Now theres a treat. (3) I remember when Bill and me went down there last year boy a trip and a half especially when we saw that giant crab I nearly fainted dead away and then there was that strange looking guy wearing a trench coat in 90 degree weather wandering around the beach gave me the creeps. (4) Bill said that his father always told him that once you get the sand in your shoes you never get it out. (5) The bugs were big tho. (6) Big bugs. (7) Nothing like around here. (8) The greatest part was learning to scuba dive. (9) Kinda scarey at first until I got the hang of it. (10) Floating around with a bunch of fish was fun. (11) It was pretty crowded thoug. (12) Lots of kids. (13) Got so crowded at the beach we finally had to get up early just to put the umbrela up and stake out a claim. (14) I wonder if my five minutes is up yet. (15) No, not quite. (16) It was warm there. (17) Hardly gets over 25 degrees up here. (18) Im tired of wearing fifty pounds of dull clothes and looking like Godzilla on a bad hair day. (19) Maybe I shoud see if Bill wants to go down there this year. (20) We could maybe even visit Disney World kinda exspensive but if I new we were going Id save my money for sure.

In reading over this piece of freewriting, at least one topic jumps out: the trip to Florida. The student now has a topic! This is the goal of freewriting. By allowing your mind to wander all over while you record the thoughts on the page, you give yourself a chance to find a topic of interest to you. Freewriting also helps with writing anxiety. Most students would feel less anxious about their writing if they knew no one would read it. Since freewriting is read only by the writer and since grammar is not a concern, it's a great way to "free" yourself from any writing anxiety. The blank page stops being public enemy #1.

So you now have two ways of **choosing a topic**: searching through your *mental encyclopedia* or *freewriting*. Other ways of finding a topic include browsing through your favorite magazines, reading the local newspaper, talking with friends and relatives, and watching television.

It's important to choose a topic that **you** will enjoy. Your writing becomes more interesting to both you and the reader.

LEVEL ONE EXERCISE #1:

On a separate sheet of paper, freewrite for five minutes. Remember, grammar doesn't count. Then underline the possible topics.

LEVEL TWO EXERCISE #1:

On a separate sheet of paper, freewrite for ten minutes. Remember, grammar doesn't count. Then underline the possible topics.

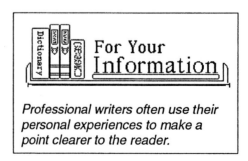

Professional writers often use their personal experiences to make a point clearer to the reader.

LEVEL ONE EXERCISE #2:

Write down at least five topics that you would enjoy writing about.

1._____

2._____

3._____

4._____

5._____

LEVEL TWO EXERCISE #2:

Write down at least ten topics that you would enjoy writing about.

1._____

2._____

3._____

4._____

5._____

6._____

7._____

8._____

9._____

10._____

1.2 Developing Ideas

When you look up a topic in the encyclopedia, you usually find quite a few details about the subject. Since you're using a mental encyclopedia, you need to find a way to get the details from your head to your paper. There are four techniques you can try; find the one that works best for you. Until you have the details on paper, it's difficult to both remember them all and organize them, too.

❏ **Focused Freewriting**

One way to **develop a topic** is called *focused freewriting*. Like regular freewriting, focused freewriting is still "free" of all grammatical restrictions, and it still has a time limit of five to ten minutes. Instead of writing whatever comes to mind, you now write whatever comes to mind **on the subject** that you have chosen. In the example used before, the writer discovered that a trip to Florida was a good topic. In the following example, the writer develops the details using focused freewriting.

Focused Freewriting Sample

(1) Lets see there was the giant crab, the huge bugs, the weird guy in the trenchcoat, the scuba diving but there was the beach whitest sand I ever saw. (2) Up here the sand is kinda dirty and grungy. (3) The water was warm. (4) There was one scare where someone yelled Shark and everybody just hightailed it outta the water. (5) The people were friendly. (6) Mostly college kids our age. (7) We shared a room with two other guys from New York City named Harry and Ted but we didn't see them much they spent their time at another hotel where there girlfriends were staying. (8) The room service was great we got shrimp scampi and lobster newberg and ate like a couple of starved pigs but it was kinda exspensive so we mostly ate hotdogs at the beach. (9)One nite we went to a bonfire on the beach everybody was sitting around listening to music roasting marshmallows and just generally dancing around in bathing suits seemed kinda weird for March to be running around in a bathing suit. (10) What else did we do oh yea there was the nite we went to one of the bars I forget the name of it but it was so crowded we left we couldn't even get near the bar. (11) by the time we got in the door we were squished like a couple of slices of ham between soggy bread. (12) We figured it wasn't worth the effort but it was a lot of fun anyways just watching all the kids from all over the place. (13) kids from California and Wisconsin, and one guy that we met from Michigan, Tim, was a fun guy. (14) He new all the outta the way places were it wasn't so crowded and we got to meet some interesting people we dont usually get to meet where we live.

❏ Listing

Another way of developing the details for a topic is to *list* all the details you can think of in whatever order they come to you, much the same way you might do a grocery list. Suppose, for example, you want to write about playing keyboards, your favorite hobby. You list all the things about the hobby.

famous	relaxing
getting the sharps and flats	learning how to strike the keys
learning the chords	buying the sheet music
singing	writing my own music
listening to tapes	getting a tutor
having fun	being popular
getting a band together	practicing two hours a day
loud	learning the notes from A to F
discipline	helps learn other instruments
irritates my sister	getting the rhythm like 2/4 time

Listing Sample

Here the details are in no particular order. The writer has looked up the hobby in the *mental encyclopedia* and copied down all the details to be found there. **The more details you can find and write down, the easier it will be to write the paragraph or essay later.** So a long list is better than a short list!

❏ Brainstorming

A third way of developing details for a topic is *brainstorming*. This time you actually pick your brain as if you were a reporter out to get a story for a newspaper. By asking yourself questions about the topic you chose, you gather details the same way a reporter does. These questions are **who, what, where, when, why,** and **how.** Some questions may not fit your topic while others may generate many details.

For example, suppose you want to write about a funny incident that happened to you when you were younger. One way to get down all the details about the incident is to answer these questions.

Who: my brother who was five, myself I was eight, my cat Southpaw, and my neighbor Fred who was in his backyard next door

What: my cat Southpaw got stuck up in a willow tree and my brother and me decided to go get it down so we got a ladder and started to climb the tree but when my brother got halfway up his pants got hung up on a broken branch and he couldn't move so he started to cry I was already up on the branch with the cat so I grabbed the cat and started to come

---

Brainstorming Sample

---

down I was almost to my brother when I dropped the cat on his head the cat just sorta stuck there on my brothers head then all of a sudden this gust of wind comes along and blows the ladder so I can't reach it by this time my brothers screaming and the cat's making funny noises Fred the guynext door sees all this and comes running over puts the ladder back up and starts to climb up to get my brother and the cat all the while my brother's crying and now Southpaws starting to hiss cause he doesn't like Fred Fred gets my brother unhooked and the cat runs down Freds back to the ground in all the comotion I lost my balance and fell on Fred and the two of us fall on the ground the last thing I remember is Fred laughing as he's telling my dad

When: summer 1956

Where: our family's backyard

Why: it was scarey at the time but when I look back on it it was pretty funny that's what a different perspective can do to an experience You tend to look back on things when you're older a different way

How: how it happened I think was because I thought at the time I could do anything and I really didn't see any dangers to me or my brother or the cat so although it seems funny now it really could have been very dangerous

Notice that with this, as with freewriting, you don't have to worry about the grammar. The main purpose is to write down everything as you think of it without worrying about spelling or punctuation or paragraphing. Again, the more you write down, the more you'll have to use for your paragraph or essay.

For Your Information

When you jot down your details quickly, be sure to write legibly so that you can read them later.

❏ Clustering

The last technique for retrieving information from your *mental encyclopedia* works best for the artistic writer. *Clustering* uses a cluster of circles or squares to map the information. Beginning with a large circle in the middle of the page, you add connected smaller circles, each with one piece of information. Circles containing similar information are grouped together with connecting lines.

For example, suppose you want to do a review of your favorite restaurant. You might begin with a large circle consisting of the restaurant's name and then add other circles with your information.

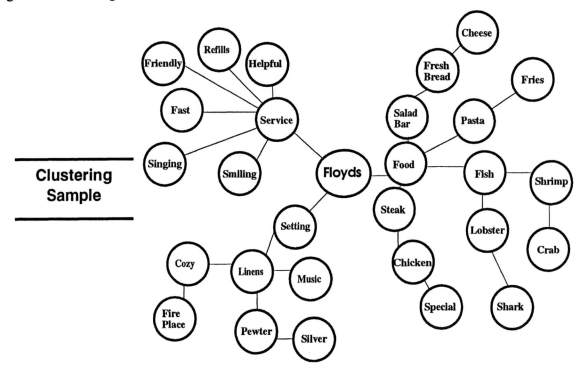

Clustering Sample

You now have four ways to copy information stored in your *mental encyclopedia: freewriting, listing, brainstorming,* and *clustering.* Try each one of them to find which one works best for you.

LEVEL ONE EXERCISE #3

Using one of the five topics from exercise #2 (page 5), **list** all the details you can on a separate sheet of paper.

LEVEL TWO EXERCISE #3

Using one of the ten topics from exercise #2 (page 5) and one of the four ways to develop a topic (**focused freewriting, listing, clustering** or **brainstorming**) write down all the details you can on a separate sheet of paper.

Chapter Two

Organizing Ideas

2.1 Organizing Paragraphs

Chronological
Space
Importance

2.2 Outlining

Roman Numeral
Decimal
Informal

KEY TERMS

Chronological .... organize a paragraph according to time

Decimal .... outline using numbers only

Importance .... organize a paragraph according to value
of ideas

Informal .... outline using headings

Outline .... system of organizing a paragraph or essay

Roman Numeral .... outline using letters and numbers

Space .... organize a paragraph according to location

2.1 Organizing Paragraphs

You have chosen your topic and developed that topic by writing down all the details. Before actually writing the paragraph or the essay, you need to organize those details so that the reader can follow them. One of the best ways to organize your details is to use an outline.

In order to make the outline work, you must first decide what order to put your details in for the body paragraph. There are three basic types of organization:

Chronological . . . . . .details are organized according to time and the order they occur
Space . . . . .details are organized according to the location they occupy
Importance . . . . .details are organized according to their importance, usually least to most

❏ Chronological Organization

In a *chronologically* organized paragraph, the events are given in the order that they occurred. The chronologically organized paragraph usually tells a story — whether a true story or a fictionalized account:

**Chronological
Paragraph**

(1) My friend Bob and I had several unusual experiences on our recent trip to Fort Lauderdale. (2) The first occurred on the flight down. (3) There was a passenger sitting across the aisle from us who had a very large basket that he insisted on holding. (4) No one thought much of it until we heard him talking into the basket. (5) The stewardess came by and said he had to put it on the top rack. (6) Eventually, we discovered he had a pet boa constrictor in the basket. (7) We were very relieved when it was moved to a separate holding area. (8) The second strange occurrence happened when we landed. (9) As we were waiting for our luggage, we saw an odd looking guy standing across the way from us. (10) He was holding a cane in one hand and an unlit cigar in the other. (11) Suddenly, a young woman approached him and put handcuffs on him. (12) We don't know what that was about, but he was smiling as he left. (13) The last occurred on the beach. (14) After we were finally settled, we decided to stroll the beach. (15) A guy with a metal detector was wandering around. (16) Then he started to jump up and down, very excited. (17) He held up a large object he had dug out of the sand. (18) After everyone gathered around someone recognized the object was an old military shell, but he thought it was a relic from paleolithic times. (19) Bob and I agreed that we'd witnessed some rather bizarre events.

❏ Spatial Organization

In a paragraph organized according to *space,* the writer is usually describing a person, place or thing. The writer decribes what he or she sees in either a clockwise or counterclockwise order:

Spatial Paragraph

(1) I knew I had wandered into the twilight zone when I entered Mary's basement bedroom. (2) The first thing I saw to the left of the door was a giant neon sign that kept flashing "Bargain Basement." (3) Underneath the sign was an old, battered chest of drawers with clothes dripping out of every drawer. (4) A ripped shirt hung down from the top, over a pair of orange socks hanging out of the second drawer, over a pair of bright green sweat pants hanging out of the bottom drawer. (5) Next to this chest was an old Victrola with the top up. (6) I could see it was missing the arm that held the needle. (7) Over the edge of the old player was a pair of stockings. (8) Across from the door, there was a window that had a bright red sheet over it, just slung over the top. (9) The bed, underneath the window, was littered with newspapers, millions of newspapers. (10) It didn't even look like a bed. (11) Next to the bed on the other side was a beat up night stand. (12) On top of the stand was a lamp without a shade and what looked like a very old banana peel. (13) On the right wall was the closet, or at least I think it was a closet. (14) It could have had several skeletons in there and no one would know because there were so many boxes of every shape and size just piled on top of each other. (15) But the real tipoff that this was no ordinary room was the automobile engine that rested on its side outside the closet door. (16) It was covered with grease and fur. (17) I decided the best thing to do was to exit before Rod Serling jumped out from under the bed.

Because the details are in a logical order, the reader can easily picture this rather disgusting room. When a writer describes a person, one of the most logical ways to organize the details is to describe the person from head to foot.

❏ Organization in Order of Importance

Organizing a paragraph in *order of importance* allows the writer to determine which of his or her details are most important and which are least important. Because a reader generally remembers the last item he or she reads, usually the least important item comes first and the most important item comes last. It's much the same as a joke; the punchline comes last!

**Importance
Paragraph**

(1) My mother taught me many valuable lessons about life. (2) She taught me to be honest and trustworthy, so that when I give my word or promise to someone that it means something. (3) I learned never to promise what I couldn't possibly deliver. (4) In return, I would earn respect. (5) As a consequence, I still have many of the friends that I had in high school. (6) My mother also believed that it was important to strive to do one's best, no matter what the job. (7) Even when I worked at McDonald's, I was always on time and I always did my best. (8) It made me feel good about myself, and it carried over to my family life and my academic life. (9) Another lesson my mother taught me was to learn from my mistakes. (10) I remember one Fourth of July when I accidently set the back porch on fire because I wasn't very careful with the matches I was using to light a sparkler. (11) I learned very quickly to pay more attention to what I was doing. (12) Another valuable lesson was being myself and not trying to be like everyone else. (13) I was always doing whatever my friends were doing until one of my friends stole some jewelry from a local store. (14) We were all arrested, but later the charges were dropped. (15) It was a hard lesson to learn, but never again did I get myself into such trouble by following the crowd. (16) The last lesson, and the most important, was to live every day to the fullest and never take anything for granted. (17) I learned to take advantage of the sunny days to do things with my family and friends and to take advantage of the days when the weather was bad by doing things that had to be done. (18) I'm glad I did because when my mother died, I had no regrets that I hadn't spent time with her to learn all she had to teach me.

Chronological, Space and *Importance* are just three of the many ways to organize the details in your body paragraphs. If your details are not logically organized, both you and the reader will have a very difficult time following them.

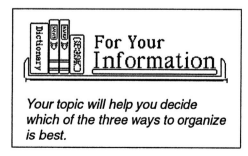

Your topic will help you decide which of the three ways to organize is best.

LEVEL ONE EXERCISE #1

Unscramble the following details by putting them in logical order.

    1. We left the movie before it was over.   _____

    2. We went to dinner before the movie.   _____

    3. We ate a box of candy before the film.   _____

    4. We bought our tickets.   _____

    5. We ate three boxes of popcorn during the previews.   _____

    6. We screamed during the middle part of the movie.   _____

    7. We went home sick.   _____

    8. We read the reviews of the movie during dinner.   _____

    9. We ordered two cheeseburgers each for dinner.   _____

    10. We vowed the next day to eat less junk food.   _____

LEVEL TWO EXERCISE #1

Decide the best organization for each of the following topics: chronological (C), spatial (S) or importance (I).

_____ an embarrassing experience   _____ reasons to eat health foods

_____ reasons for choosing a four year college   _____ causes of civil unrest

_____ description of presidential elections   _____ how to sell cars

_____ ways to succeed in college   _____ advantages of higher education

_____ results of civil disobedience   _____ steps in getting a job

_____ description of an unusual place   _____ results of prejudice

_____ how to tell a joke   _____ results of affirmative action

2.2 Outlining

Now that you have found your topic, developed your topic and determined the best way to organize the details, the next step is to outline your paragraph or essay. This is your blueprint to make writing the paragraph or essay easier.

There are two types of formal outlines: *the **Roman numeral** outline* and *the decimal outline*.

In the Roman numeral outline, numbers and letters are used to represent each part of the essay or paragraph. In the decimal outline, only numbers are used to represent the same parts. The *informal outline* uses no numbers or letters. Because each essay must have an introduction, body, and conclusion, the outline is arranged by its sections. (See Chapter Six) To outline a paragraph, you need use only the body paragraph section of the outline.

Roman numeral	Decimal	Informal
I. Introduction	1.0 Introduction	Introduction
A. Opening Remark	1.1 Opening Remark	Opening Remark
B. Thesis Statement	1.2 Thesis Statement	Thesis Statement
II. Body Paragraph	2.0 Body Paragraph	Body Paragraph
A. Topic Sentence	2.1 Topic Sentence	Topic Sentence
B. Details	2.2 Details	Details
1.	2.2.1	1
2.	2.2.2	2
3.	2.2.3	3
4.	2.2.4	4
5.	2.2.5	5
6.	2.2.6	6
7.	2.2.7	7
8.	2.2.8	8
9.	2.2.9	9
III. Conclusion	3.0 Conclusion	Conclusion
A. Restatement of Thesis	3.1 Restatement of Thesis	Restatement of Thesis
B. Concluding Remarks	3.2 Concluding Remarks	Concluding Remarks

For example, the chronologically organized paragraph on page 11 was outlined using the *Roman numeral* outline:

II. Body Paragraph
   A. Topic Sentence: unusual experiences on trip to Fort Lauderdale
   B. Details:

**Roman Numeral
Sample**

       1. first on flight down
       2. passenger with large basket
       3. refused to put on rack
       4. boa constrictor
       5. second at landing
       6. odd looking guy
       7. handcuffed by young woman
       8. third on beach
       9. guy with metal detector
     10. military shell

Remember that you don't want the outlining to take forever. Jot down just enough words to remember what details you want to include in the order you want to include them. Once you have your listing, brainstorming, clustering or freewriting done, you write the outline to organize the details you have.

Now you have a plan to write your paragraph or essay. With this plan, the writing becomes easier, and the reading becomes clearer. You know where you are starting, where you are going, and where you are ending. While planning takes time, it helps the writer stay on track, helps the writing become easier, and helps the reader understand the material.

For Your **Information**

*Use words and phrases rather than
sentences in your outlines.*

LEVEL ONE EXERCISE #2:

(1) Choose one of the following topic sentences or make up one of your own. (2) Jot down all the details you can. (3) Then put those details into the outline form provided.

(1) **Choose one:**

1. Topic Sentence: There are several attributes a student should possess to succeed in college.

2. Topic Sentence: Education can help improve relationships between different people.

3. Topic Sentence: (one of your own)

   _____

(2) **Jot down details:**

1. _____   5. _____

2. _____   6. _____

3. _____   7. _____

4. _____   8. _____

(3) **Organize details:**

Topic Sentence _____

Details (organized chronologically, spatially, or by importance)

1. _____

2. _____

3. _____

4. _____

5. _____

6. _____

7. _____

8. _____

LEVEL TWO EXERCISE #2:

Using the details from Exercise #3 on page 9 in Chapter One, outline your essay below.

I. Introduction

    A. Hook _____

    B. Thesis _____

II. Body

    A. Topic Sentence _____

    B. Details:

        1. _____

        2. _____

        3. _____

        4. _____

        5. _____

        6. _____

        7. _____

        8. _____

        9. _____

        10. _____

        11. _____

        12. _____

III. Conclusion

    A. Restatement of Thesis _____

    B. Concluding Remark _____

Chapter Three

The Body Paragraph

3.1 Topic Sentence

Subject and Aspect

3.2 Specific, Supporting Details

3.3 Transitions

Definition
Types

KEY TERMS

Body Paragraph.. contains information on one aspect
of a subject

Specific Detail .... specific piece of information

Topic Sentence.. contains the subject and the aspect

Transition.. words that connect ideas or sentences
in a paragraph

Without the ***body paragraph***, there is no essay! All the information you wish to give the reader is going into this paragraph. **The body paragraph's primary purpose is to discuss one aspect in detail.** When you take a picture with the zoom lens of a camera, you focus on one small object. You want the reader to have a clear, sharp picture of what you see. If you shift your focus, you need a new body paragraph to contain the details of the next picture.

Each **body paragraph** has a **topic sentence, supporting details,** and **transitions.**

3.1 The Topic Sentence

The **Topic Sentence** lets the reader know the subject of the paragraph. It's usually the first sentence of the paragraph.

❑ **Subject and Aspect**

Generally, the topic sentence consists of the **subject** plus the **aspect** of the subject to be discussed. For example, if your subject were body building, your aspect might be the physical effects of the sport. Think of the topic sentence as your road sign to the reader: the subject and the aspect of this paragraph are _____ and _____. The clearer your topic sentence, the easier it will be for the reader to follow along. Here are some sample topic sentences with the subject in italics and the aspect in bold:

> *Body building is a sport* **designed to increase muscle tone.**
>   subject   aspect

> *A college education is necessary* **for an entry level position in banking.**
>   subject   aspect

> **Writing better cover letters is one advantage** of the *personal computer.*
>   aspect   subject

A clear topic sentence not only helps the reader identify precisely the content of the paragraph, but also helps you, the writer, stay on track. You don't want to veer off the road by discussing something else in the paragraph. Using your prewriting will help you steer the paragraph in one direction.

For example, suppose your subject is the movie *Dances with Wolves.* The body paragraph can't discuss *all* the aspects of the movie from the set design to the characters to the plot to the theme to the cinematography. You need to narrow your focus to one specific aspect such as the portrayal of the Native Americans. You may decide on a topic sentence that says,"The portrayal of Native Americans in the movie *Dances with Wolves* is realistic." Now both you and the reader know exactly what the paragraph concerns. You can use your listing, brainstorming, clustering or freewriting to develop the details.

LEVEL ONE EXERCISE #1

Rewrite the following topic sentences to make the subject and the aspect more specific.

1. Education is important.

_____

2. Stress is harmful.

_____

3. People should change their eating habits.

_____

4. Reading is good.

_____

5. Sports help children.

_____

LEVEL TWO EXERCISE #1

On a separate sheet of paper, create a topic sentence for each of the following subjects:

1. Education	6. Children
2. Hobbies	7. Vacations
3. Values	8. Exercise
4. Music	9. Jobs
5. Friends	10. Family

3.2 Specific, Supporting Details

Once you have your **topic sentence**, you're now ready to provide the reader with all the information on the subject of the body paragraph. Your prewriting and your outline should contain all the information you need to make the body paragraph substantial, but you may want to touch up the details.

The details you include in the body paragraph should be **specific**. If you take a fuzzy picture with a camera, you may find it difficult to distinguish Aunt Berta from Uncle Frank. If the details in the body paragraph are fuzzy — or too general — the reader is going to have a difficult time determining what it is you mean.

In the sentence, "There is an animal on your roof," the word *animal* is far too general for the reader to get the picture. But if it said, "There is a *rhinocerous* on your roof," the reader will have a very definite (and weird) picture. Each sentence of the body paragraph should contain specific details so that the reader will have a specific picture in his or her head.

Each detail should also **support** the topic sentence. In other words, all the details should be about the aspect and only that aspect contained in the topic sentence. If you were writing about the food at your favorite restaurant, all the details in the paragraph should be about the food. Any details about the singing waitresses and waiters, the moose head on the wall, or the exotic plants would have to wait for their own paragraphs.

For example, notice how the details in the following paragraph are specific and support the topic sentence. The topic sentence is in italics.

Sample Paragraph

(1) *There are several ways to learn how to use a personal computer.* (2) One of the easiest ways to learn how to operate a personal computer is to install several games. (3) Games can help the novice learn how to use the mouse, the keyboard, and the commands. (4) For example, the game Solitaire, available with a program called Windows, is exactly like the card game. (5) The player uses the keyboard to access the game, the mouse to move the cards, and the keyboard to change commands. (6) Another way to learn how to use a personal computer is to take a course at a local high school or college. (7) These courses are offered in both day and evening divisions and often run only a few weeks. (8) They are usually inexpensive and can help the novice understand basic functions. (9)The third, and most expensive, way to learn how to operate a personal computer is to buy the computer and hire a computer expert to demonstrate its uses. (10) Because each person's needs for the computer are different, it may be faster to learn with an expert who can

tailor the computer to the person's needs. (11) It is also possible to learn how to use a computer by simply reading the manuals that come with the various programs. (12) However, this "trial and error" method may take the longest and be the most frustrating. (13) With so many ways to master the personal computer, everyone should become computer literate.

The topic sentence, sentence #1, lets us know that this paragraph is about the subject personal computers and the aspect concerns the ways to learn how to use one. Each sentence that follows develops that aspect with specific details that support the topic sentence. The writer makes sure the reader understands the various ways to become computer literate.

LEVEL ONE AND LEVEL TWO EXERCISE #2

Identify each of the following words as general (G) or specific (S).

_____1. tree

_____2. Alaska

_____3. football

_____4. movie

_____5. Chicago

_____6. food

_____7. building

_____8. crime

_____9. hog calling contest

_____10. buttered popcorn

_____11. sports

_____12. rose

_____13. elm tree

_____14. city

_____15. *Dances With Wolves*

_____16. flower

_____17. cheese and pepperoni pizza

_____18. Empire State Building

_____19. event

_____20. state

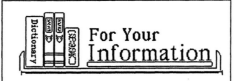

A clear topic sentence helps both the writer and the reader — make it a clear shot!

LEVEL ONE EXERCISE #3

Read the following paragraph and on the lines provided, put the numbers of the sentences that do not support the topic sentence.

(1) The food at the Chicken Palace is mouth-watering. (2) The chicken is roasted over a pit so the juices stay in, making it succulent and tasty. (3) It comes with a choice of baked potato or french fries. (4) The waitresses are very friendly, and they serve their customers promptly. (5) The sauce that comes with the chicken is spicy and can be used for the chicken or the fries. (6) The atmosphere is comfortable since there are mostly booths with both smoking and nonsmoking sections. (7) There are also several salads; the Caesar salad comes with the Palace's special dressing and is particularly creamy. (8) Generally, there is some background music, but it's not obtrusive. (9) The speciality dessert is lemon meringue pie with tangy lemon on a soft pie crust. (10) The hot fudge sundae is also a treat for the discriminating palate. (11) Prices are reasonable; a family of four can eat a full course meal for under $25. (12) My family usually goes to the Chicken Palace on Friday nights.

     1._____   2._____   3._____   4._____

LEVEL TWO EXERCISE #3

On a separate sheet of paper, write a paragraph using one of the topic sentences you wrote for exercise #1. Be sure to do the prewriting first.

3.3 Transitions

Transitions are words that connect the ideas and prevent the reader from getting lost in your paragraph. In a way, transitions are like road signs. If you wanted to give someone directions to your house, you'd tell them the main routes and which way to turn on each route. You wouldn't want to name every street they might encounter or give too few of the main routes. Transitions let the reader know where he or she is in the paragraph, but you don't want so many that you'll confuse them or so few that they'll be lost.

There are many words that act as transitions. This chart includes some of the more common transitions and the ways they connect ideas.

❑ **Types**

Addition	**Cause and Effect**	**Contrast**
(one idea added to another)	(one idea causing another or resulting from another)	(two contrasting ideas)
also	accordingly	conversely
furthermore	as a consequence	however
in addition	as a result	nevertheless
moreover	consequently	nonetheless
plus	therefore	on the other hand
	thus	

Example	**Time**
(example follows)	(two ideas related by time)
for example	afterwards
to illustrate	finally
	first
	following
	next
	second
	subsequently
	then

Another type of transition includes *repetition of key words or phrases* throughout the paragraph. This, however, is a bit tricky. Supposing you want to hammer home the point that a pig is large. You could repeat the word large, but you run the risk of putting the reader into a deep sleep. A better choice might be to use synonyms — words that mean the same. So, instead of repeating large, you could use words like *enormous, massive, heavy, big, humungous, giant, grand,* etc.

The bottom line is to keep the reader from getting lost in your paragraph, you need *enough* transitions so the reader can follow your ideas easily.

The following paragraph has the transitions in italics.

Transitions Paragraph

(1) There are several key points to a good resume. (2) The *first* point is to make sure all the information is provided. (3) *For example*, you need to be sure to have your name, address, and telephone number at the top of the resume. (4) *In addition*, you want to include your educational background and job descriptions, beginning with the last degree and job and moving down to the first. (5) The *second* point is to be neat. (6) *Neatness* counts, especially with the competition in the job market. (7) If you do not type yourself, you want to hire someone to do it for you. (8) There are *also* companies that do resumes for you for a small fee. (9) The *last* point is to include a cover letter with the *resume*. (10) This *letter* should sell yourself to the employer by emphasizing the skills you have for the job and the reasons you are the best person for the position. (11) *In addition*, if you were referred to the company by an employee, you should mention the person's name. (12) A good *resume* makes an good introduction to a prospective employer.

The *body paragraph* is much like a snapshot of information. The **topic sentence** is like the caption on the picture that summarizes for the reader the information provided. The **details** must be **specific** and must **support** the topic sentence: each detail is one portion of the larger picture, so each one must be clear, concise and relevant. **Transitions** help connect the ideas to one another so that the reader can follow the ideas. After reading the paragraph, the reader should have a clear picture in his or her mind of exactly what you mean.

A fuzzy topic sentence with even fuzzier details will leave the reader wondering what you were trying to say. **Remember:** your job as the writer is to make your subject clear and the information you provide interesting.

Make the details clear and bright!

LEVEL ONE EXERCISE #4

Insert transitions in the lines provided.

(1) To succeed in college, a student should possess three attributes. (2) The _____ attribute is determination. (3) Without _____, homework will not get done, classes will be missed and notes will not be taken. (4)_____, determination helps me do my calculus homework. (5) Since I have trouble in _____, I usually don't want to do the homework because it is time-consuming and difficult. (6) My _____ helps me accomplish this goal. (7) The _____ attribute is discipline. (8) Getting to class on time, taking accurate notes, and getting extra help when needed requires _____. (9) The _____ attribute is curiosity. (10) Learning is interesting if the student takes an active role in his studies. (11)_____, I always look up new words I find in my text books, look for articles on new information, and ask questions when I'm confused about a subject. (12) These _____ attributes can help a student have a successful college career and carry over to the job market.

LEVEL TWO EXERCISE #4

Copy a short, interesting paragraph out of one of your textbooks and underline the transitions.

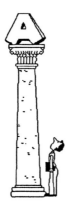

Chapter Four

Introduction

4.1 Opening Remark - Hook

Anecdote
Definition
Question
Quotation
Refutation
Startling Statement
Vivid Sketch

4.2 Thesis Statement

Subject and Aspects

KEY TERMS

Aspect .... perspective on subject contained in the thesis statement

Anecdote .... short story to begin an essay

Definition .... definition of an important term to begin an essay

Opening Remark .... first sentence of the essay

Question .... a question relative to the topic to begin an essay

Quotation .... famous or invented quotation to begin an essay

Refutation .... a general statement and disagreement to begin an essay

Startling Statement .... a sentence containing unusual information to begin an essay

Subject .... the primary part of a thesis statement

Thesis .... the main subject of the essay

Generally, when a person is called into a company for a job interview, the potential employee wants to make a good first impression. A person who applies for a job at a bank by showing up for the interview in tattered shorts and a ripped tank top is not going to make a very favorable impression on the potential employer. In fact, it may be the shortest interview on record.

The first paragraph of an essay is similar to that job interview. You as the writer want to make a favorable first impression on the reader. Remember that the reader is under no obligation to read the entire essay unless he or she is interested. Your job as the writer is to make the reader interested. So the first paragraph or introduction is crucial. If you lose the reader here, the reader will miss all your wonderful knowledge contained in the rest of the essay.

The **introduction** has two main parts. The first part is the **opening remark** which may have more than one sentence. The second part is the **thesis statement** which tells the reader not only the subject of your essay, but also the aspects.

4.1 The Opening Remark

Here's where you must "hook" the reader — get the reader so interested that he or she will want to continue reading your essay. The opening remark is usually the first sentence, though it may contain more than one sentence. It does not have to be the first sentence you write! Often, students have trouble getting started, even when they have excellent outlines. That first sentence may not come to you right away, but there are some different categories of opening remarks that may help you draft that all important first sentence. No matter which one you choose, the opening remark should lead to your thesis statement. In each example below, the thesis statement is underlined.

❏ **Anecdote** is a very short story, generally no more than two or three sentences. The story should be relevant to your topic.

> *I was lost. There seemed to be a maze of sidewalks and buildings, so I stood where I was on the verge of hysteria. Suddenly, a young man dressed in jeans and a sweater tapped me on the shoulder and asked if he could help. The friendliness of this student helped me decide to choose this college.* <u>The location, small classes and low tuition made this college the best choice for me.</u>

❏ **Definition** is either a dictionary definition or a personal definition of a key term in your essay. This definition should help the reader understand your perspective on your subject.

> *Ignorance is a cancer that destroys growth and kills the spirit. Because I was determined to combat this disease in myself, I decided to return to college.* <u>This college was the best choice because of its curricula, its low tuition and its excellent teaching staff.</u>

❑ **Question** is often used to begin an essay — sometimes too often, so be careful choosing this type of opening remark. You want to ask a question that the reader may find interesting, not a question that is too general such as "What do you think about racism?" One of the primary differences between speaking and writing is the lack of immediate interaction between two people. When you're talking to someone, you might just ask such a question, but you expect an answer. In written work, a question such as this can't be answered directly. So the question you use should be imaginative, thought-provoking, and still lead to your thesis.

> *Where can you find rock music, Shakespeare, drafting tables, computers, and Freud?* This college has these and much more, but I chose this college for its location, small classes and low tuition.

❑ **Quotation** is another way of opening an essay. The quotation may be a famous one such as you might find in *Bartlett's Quotations* or it may be one that you invent. In both cases, the punctuation is the tricky part. Briefly, there are two parts to a quotation — the actual words of the person and the dialogue tag that tells the reader who's speaking. The actual words are always in quotation marks and are usually separated from the dialogue tag by a comma.

"Actual Words of the person," dialogue tag. *(notice the comma comes before the last set of quotation marks)*
Dialogue tag, "Actual Words of the person." *(notice the period comes before the last set of quotation marks)*
"Part of the actual words of the person," dialogue tag, "and the rest of the actual words." *(called a split quotation)*

> *"Going to the University is like going to a daily freak show where all you learn is how to overcome fear of crowds,"* *my older sister warned me.* So, I chose this college because of the small classes, low tuition and friendly students.

❑ **Refutation** means to contradict and a refutation used as an opening begins with a general statement with which the author disagrees.

> *Nearly everyone believes quality has to be expensive. I disagree.* I found quality education at this college where small classes, excellent teachers and superb placement are the norm.

❑ **Startling Statement** is a sentence that may shock the reader, or surprise the reader, or puzzle the reader. Its primary intent is to wake up the reader. It often ends with an exclamation point to make the statement even more emphatic.

> *This college should be boycotted — unless you're looking*
> *for a quality education at a reasonable price!* <u>This college</u>
> <u>has small classes, excellent teachers and low tuition.</u>

❑ **Vivid Sketch** is a short description of something relevant to your topic. Again, you want this to be brief but interesting by choosing specific details.

> *The pale green walls seem stark under the fluorescent*
> *lights, but the atmosphere is warm, curious and vibrant with*
> *learning at this college.* <u>The location, small classes and low</u>
> <u>tuition made this the best college for me.</u>

      The **anecdote, definition question, quotation, refutation, startling statement,** and **vivid sketch** are only a few of the many ways to start an essay so that the reader is "hooked" into reading the rest of the essay. You may also mix and match any of these. The bottom line is that the opening sentence or sentences must capture the reader's attention. You want to make sure the reader doesn't take a short nap, so draft the opening carefully, even if you must draft it *after* you've written the rest of the essay.

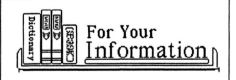

Generally, on an essay exam, an opening is not as important as the information in the body paragraphs.

LEVEL ONE EXERCISE #1

Explain why each of the following openings needs revision.

1.   Electricity is what carries light to millions of people.

2.   Humans are different from apes.

3.   I like fishing.

4.   Going to the movies is fun.

5.   Do you like "The Flintstones"?

6.   Broccoli is good for you.

7.   Everyone should exercise.

8.   Cats are different than dogs.

9.   Eating tacos gives me indigestion.

10.   People should learn to like each other.

LEVEL TWO EXERCISE #1

Using the following subjects, write an opening using the type named:

1.   Racism *(Definition)*

2.   Politics *(Quotation)*

3.   Television *(Refutation)*

4.   Sports *(Anecdote)*

5.   Music *(Startling Statement)*

4.2 The Thesis Statement

❑ **Subject and Aspects**

Unlike the **topic sentence** that we looked at in Chapter Three (page 20), the **thesis** provides the reader with a clear understanding of the **subject** and the *all* of the **aspects** of that subject to be discussed in the *entire* essay. The topic sentence of the body paragraph gives the subject and one aspect for that one body paragraph only.

The thesis statement in each of the examples of opening remarks (pages 29 - 31)provides the **subject** (the college the student is attending) and several different **aspects** (low tuition, small classes, excellent teachers, excellent curricula, friendly students). In writing a thesis and support essay, or basic composition, it's easier for both the writer and the reader if the aspects are named. **Each aspect will become the topic of a separate body paragraph.**

Examples of Thesis Statements:

1. **A sense of humor** can help *overcome adversity* and *increase popularity*.
   subject   aspect #1   aspect #2

2. **Relaxation techniques** include *meditation, breathing exercises* and *imaging*.
   subject   aspect #1   aspect #2   aspect #3

3. **An herbal garden** is *easy to design* and *maintain*.
   subject   aspect #1   aspect #2

4. **Drunk drivers** *should have their licenses revoked* and *serve jail time* .
   subject   aspect #1   aspect #2

5. *Job experience*, *money* and *maturity* are reasons **to wait before going to college.**
   aspect #1   aspect #2   aspect #3   subject

The clearer the thesis statement is, the easier it will be for the writer to write the essay and for the reader to follow it. **The number of aspects given in the thesis statement will determine the number of body paragraphs.** For example, in number 1 above, there are two aspects, so the essay will have two body paragraphs: the first body paragraph will discuss the first aspect (overcoming adversity) and the second paragraph will discuss the second aspect (increasing popularity). Number 5 has three aspects, and so the essay will have three paragraphs, each dealing with one of the aspects. In this way, your thesis statement, if it's clearly written, is much like a mini-outline for the reader.

The **opening remark** and the **thesis statement** together form the entire introduction. If the opening remark is interesting and the thesis statement is clear, you have the reader hooked.

LEVEL ONE EXERCISE #2

Revise each of the following thesis statements. You may change whatever you wish to arrive at a clear thesis statement for each one.

      1.   Eating junk food is bad for your health.

      2.   Jogging is good.

      3.   Fort Lauderdale is interesting.

      4.   Politicians are crooks.

      5.   Going to the dentist is yucky.

LEVEL TWO EXERCISE #2

Revise each of the following thesis statements. You may change whatever you wish to make the thesis clear and concise.

      1.   Sports may be harmful to young children.

      2.   There is too much violence on television.

      3.   The rating system for movies needs to be revised.

      4.   Students should not be penalized for absences.

      5.   Racism is a problem everywhere.

      6.   Abortion is a controversial issue.

      7.   Everyone should exercise every day.

      8.   A college degree is necessary in today's job market.

      9.   The value of money has changed over the years.

    10.   Parents should teach their children good values.

LEVEL ONE EXERCISE #3

Write five thesis statements on subjects of your choosing. Underline the subject once and underline each of the aspects twice.

1.

_____

_____

2.

_____

_____

3.

_____

_____

4.

_____

_____

5.

_____

_____

LEVEL TWO EXERCISE #3

On a separate sheet of paper, write five introductions using your topics from Chapter One. Use your prewriting to help you. Be sure each has an opening remark and a clear thesis statement.

Chapter Five

Conclusion

5.1 Restatement of theThesis

Subject and Aspects

5.2 Concluding Remark

Prediction
Question
Quotation
Recommendation
Relevant example

KEY TERMS

Concluding Remarks ....last sentence or sentences

Conclusion...............................last paragraph of an essay

Prediction ....a forecast about the future of the subject

Question ....a final question that the reader can ponder

Quotation ....a famous or invented quotation that ends the essay

Recommendation.......................a suggestion that the reader take action

Relevant Example ....another example of the subject of the essay

Restatement of the thesis............usually the first sentence of the conclusion

Most of us have a tendency to remember best what we hear, see, or read last. As a result, the **conclusion** is one of the most important paragraphs. The conclusion is the last paragraph of the essay — the reader will remember it. If the conclusion is weak, the reader will not be impressed with the essay.

The **conclusion** is your last opportunity as a writer to emphasize not only the subject and the aspects, but also the importance of these to the reader. This is also your opportunity to reach out to the reader and make the information you've presented as relevant to the reader as possible. Why should the reader be interested in what you've had to say? Your job as the writer is to make the essay relevant to the reader by providing a connection between the subject of your essay and the reader of your essay.

The **conclusion** contains a **restatement of the thesis** with both the subject and aspects repeated and a **concluding remark** of one or more sentences designed to leave the reader thinking about the information presented in the essay.

5.1 Restatement of the Thesis

Because your essay of thesis and support is relatively short, there really is no need for a summary. You may have from one to three or four body paragraphs that the reader can easily reread. For a longer essay or for a research paper, a summary is necessary because the reader may have forgotten one or two of the main points by the time he or she reaches the end of the essay. Here, however, you need only remind the reader of the subject and the aspects.

❑ **Subject and Aspects**

Usually the **restatement of the thesis** is the first sentence of the conclusion and repeats the **subject** and the **aspects** using different words than those you used in the initial thesis statement in the introduction. After all, the reader doesn't want to read the same sentence twice.

Here is one of the thesis statements from the previous chapter on introductions:

I chose this college because of the *location*, *small classes* and *low tuition*.
      subject   aspect #1   aspect #2   aspect #3

For the restatement, the subject and the aspects must remain the same, but the wording should alter:

The *location*, *small classes* and *low tuition* are the main reasons I **chose to attend this college**.
    aspect #1   aspect #2   aspect #3   subject

The writer has the chance to repeat the aspects and the subject, while the reader reads a new sentence to remind him or her of what the body paragraphs contained. Here are a few more examples:

1

ORIGINAL THESIS: The *condition*, *age*, and *origin* of stamps **determine their price.**

RESTATEMENT: As you can see, when the *condition* is mint, the *age* is pre-modern, and the *origin* is exotic, **the price of stamps increases.**

2

ORIGINAL THESIS: **Going to college** *helped me mature, learn more about electronics* and *make new friends.*

RESTATEMENT: **Since I started college,** *I have been more responsible, learned about the intricacies of electronics* and *met Frank and Joan.*

3

ORIGINAL THESIS: *Eating low cholesterol foods* and *exercising* have **made me feel better.**

RESTATEMENT: **My health has improved** since I started *eating foods low in cholesterol,* especially increasing my intake of vegetables, and since I started on *a moderate exercise program* of aerobics every day.

4

ORIGINAL THESIS: **Prejudice** can occur in many forms, including *housing discrimination* and *substandard service.*

RESTATEMENT: *Being unable to purchase a home in any area* and *receiving poor service* are only two of the many forms **prejudice** can take.

5

ORIGINAL THESIS: **Finding a job** requires *perseverance, appearance* and *opportunity.*

RESTATEMENT: If you constantly *pursue every possibility, maintain a neat resume and neat appearance,* and *seize every opportunity to network,* you are more likely to be successful in **finding a job.**

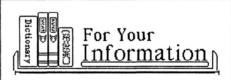

For Your
Information

It's a good idea to keep the aspects in the same order they are discussed to maintain logic.

LEVEL ONE EXERCISE #1

Rewrite each of the following original thesis statements:

1. A resume should include personal information, job experience and educational background.

_____

_____

2. Getting the proper amount of rest, eating well, and exercising can help a student study better.

_____

_____

3. Three popular cartoons are "The Flintstones," "Mutant Ninja Turtles," and "Bugs Bunny."

_____

_____

4. A personal computer can help balance a budget and organize recipes.

_____

_____

5. A career in teaching is personally rewarding and financially secure.

_____

_____

LEVEL TWO EXERCISE #1

Using the introductions written in Chapter Four (page 35), change each of your thesis statements to restatements.

5.2 CONCLUDING REMARK

The **concluding remark** is the last sentence (or sentences) of your essay. Now is not the time to nod off. This is the time for the BIG FINISH, almost like the punchline to a joke. This is what the reader will remember, and if it's not very memorable, all your hard work up to this point can be compromised. Like the opening remark in the introduction, the concluding remark must still interest the reader. You want the reader to think about what you've had to say, long after they've finished reading the essay.

As there were types of introductory remarks to get the essay started, so there are types of concluding remarks to help you end the essay. The restatement of the thesis is underlined in each one of the samples below.

❏ **Prediction:** Based on what you had to say about your subject in the body paragraphs, you may now look into your crystal ball and predict what will happen to your subject in the future.

> <u>Therefore, the location, small classes and low tuition helped me chose this college.</u> *Once the community discovers the quality education available here, more and more people will take advantage of the opportunities offered by this institution.*

❏ **Question:** As you could begin your essay with the question, so you can end an essay with a question. The same stipulations apply, however. You don't want the question to be boring, such as "What do you think?" You want the question to lead the reader to examine his or her own thoughts about the subject. (See Chapter four, page 30)

> <u>Location, small classes and low tuition make the college the best choice.</u> *Why not find out for yourself just how inexpensive a quality education can be by visiting your local community college?*

❏ **Quotation:** The quotation can also be used as both an opening remark and a closing remark, but again, the punctuation must be accurate. Quotation marks go around the actual words of the person, and the dialogue tag — who is speaking — is set apart by a comma. It need not be famous, but it should be relevant to the subject. (See Chapter Four, page 30)

> <u>In conclusion, the location, small classes, and low tuition make the choice easy for me.</u> *As I saw on a poster once, "The larger the island of knowledge, the shorter the shoreline of wonder." Enroll at your local community college and wonder no more.*

❏ **Recommendation:** Using this type of concluding remark, you can suggest that the reader do something relative to the subject. Depending on how emphatic you want to make this suggestion, it can be either subtle or quite blatant.

> The location, small classes, and low tuition are the three reasons I chose this college. *I recommend that anyone who's looking for a quality education come to this college and discover the benefits of a community college.*

❏ **Relevant Example:** The example that you choose for this need not be long, but it does have to be relevant to the subject discussed in the body paragraphs. This type of closing is particularly effective if you have already used examples in your body paragraphs.

> So, I chose this college because of its location, small classes and low tuition. *After having attended the large university in the area for one semester where the classes have over five hundred students and the tuition is nearly $12,000 a year, I can truly say that this college offers a quality education at an affordable price.*

As you can see in the last example, you may mix and match the concluding remarks as well. The last example contains both a quotation and a recommendation. **Prediction, question, quotation, recommendation,** and **relevant example** are a few of the many ways to end your essay so that it packs a punch.

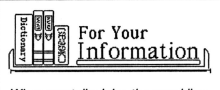

For Your Information

When you tell a joke, the punchline comes at the end. The end of an essay should pack a punch, too.

Four Problems to be Avoided

There are a few pitfalls that plague conclusions and should be avoided.

(1) Wordy Conclusions: There's no need to beat the reader over the head with the fact that he or she is reading the conclusion. Clearly, if it's the last paragraph, it must be the conclusion. Avoid wordy conclusion tags such as "In conclusion, I would just like to close by saying...." A simple transition such as *therefore, so, finally* is sufficient.

(2) New Material: Often, a student reaches the conclusion and suddenly remembers information that was not on his or her outline, but which he or she wanted to include. Now is not the time to throw it in. The reader is expecting the writer to be finished with all information. Putting new information in the conclusion suggests that the essay really isn't over. The new material should be included in the body paragraph where it most appropriately fits, but never include it in the conclusion.

(3) Change in Tone: Occasionally, a writer may inadvertently change the tone of the essay in the conclusion. If, for example, the essay has been dealing seriously with a subject, it's expected that the serious tone will be maintained through the conclusion. Throwing in a joke will confuse the reader. Unless there's a good reason to change the tone, it's best to be consistent.

(4) Repeated Thesis: If the thesis is repeated word for word in the restatement, the reader will be bored. The writer needs to insure some variety by changing the words while keeping the same subject and aspects. Life is too short to read the same sentence twice.

Now that you have completed your **conclusion** with a **restatement of the thesis** and **concluding remarks,** your first draft (rough draft) is finished. Now is the time to check it over for organizational problems or for grammatical errors. (See Chapter Six, Postwriting, page 49)

LEVEL ONE EXERCISE #2

Identify the type of concluding remark in each of the following examples. Some have more than one type.

1.   So, three beers impaired my judgement and slowed my reflexes. My friend Eliot wasn't so lucky. After he had a few drinks at our local hangout, he lost control of his van and rammed a bridge abutment. He was dead on arrival at the hospital. If we drink and drive, our lives are ever in danger.

_____

2.   Nursing is a rewarding career with both personal benefits and financial rewards. I suggest that you choose a career field by taking an aptitude test and talking to those already in the career you might like to enter.

_____

3.   The old television shows like "The Ed Sullivan Show," "The Jackie Gleason Show," and "The Dinah Shore Show" provided wonderful entertainment. It's unfortunate that these types of shows with such great talents and wholesome family viewing will never be seen again.

_____

4.   The seasons of some sports are too long, too expensive and too boring. As I heard an announcer say, "Hockey was never meant to be played after the ice melts and baseball was never meant to be played with snow on the field."

_____

5.   Sammy's Drive-in Taco Stand has the worst food, the worst service and the worst atmosphere of any restaurant in the continental United States. Why would anyone risk ptomaine poisoning at a place that should be condemned by the health department?

_____

LEVEL TWO EXERCISE #2

Write concluding remarks for the restatements you wrote in Exercise #1 (page 39). Be sure to chose the most effective closing for each one.

Chapter Six

PUTTING THE ESSAY TOGETHER

6.1 INTRODUCTION, BODY, CONCLUSION

6.2 POSTWRITING

6.3 WRITING WORKSHOP

6.4 TOPIC CHOICES

6.1 Introduction, Body, Conclusion

We have discussed all the parts to an essay:

Introduction

Opening Remark
Thesis Statement

Body

Topic Sentence
Specific, Supporting Details

Conclusion

Restatement of the Thesis
Concluding Remarks

A graphic representation might look something like this:

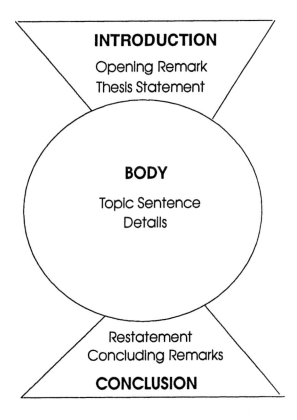

Here are two examples of student essays with each of the parts marked.

Essay by John Boeckel

Essay by John Boeckel

OPENING REMARKS

(1) Man has had a fascination with flight ever since he first witnessed birds soaring in the sky. (2) I have always wanted to learn to fly a small plane myself, but the high cost of instruction has put this idea out of my reach. (3) My only alternative was to get into flying in a much smaller scale. (4) I decided to try **Radio Control Model Aviation** as a less expensive

THESIS STATEMENT

alternative, and found it to be an *exciting* and *educational* experience.

TOPIC SENTENCE

(5) **Flying radio controlled model airplanes** can be an *exciting* experience. (6) Model planes have a lot of similarities to full-sized aircraft, but they cost only a fraction of what one would have to spend for a full-sized plane. (7) Although you are not going to get a ride in a model plane, you will sometimes feel as if you are in the cockpit while you stand on the ground controlling all of its movements. (8) Model planes have almost all of the same control functions as their full-sized counterparts,

SUPPORTING DETAILS

and you really have to keep yourself focused to keep your plane under control. (9) Even after several years of flying R.C. planes, my heart still beats out of control when I perform high-speed maneuvers close to the ground. (10) R.C. planes are normally very light, and gusts or shifts of the wind can have a devastating effect on an R.C. plane and your heart. (11) Takeoffs and landings are probably the most exciting parts of flying because of the high speeds needed to achieve lift and the plane being so close to the ground. (12) This is one good way to feel some of the excitement of flying without spending a small fortune.

TOPIC SENTENCE

(13) **Flying radio control planes** can also be an *educational* experience. (14) There are many aspects of flying that you must learn and understand before you can fly. (15) Most model planes are built from precut kits, and if you follow the instructions carefully when assembling your plane, it will probably fly. (16) I have learned that proper wing and stabilizer

alignment is very important if you want the maximum handling characteristics out of your plane. (17) It is also important to have the control surfaces such as the rudder, elevator, and ailerons hinged close and straight, or they will lose efficiency and cause excessive drag. (18) Balance, I also learned, is another factor that affects a plane's handling and performance. (19) If the plane's center of gravity is not at the thickest part of the wing where the most lift is generated, you will constantly have to control the plane's altitude with the elevator which can become increasingly difficult especially when you are taking off or landing. (20) I found that it was necessary to learn something about electronics since the plane is controlled by radio waves actuating miniature electronic robotic servos. (21) Believe it or not this hobby can even become a career. (22) Hollywood movie productions make full use of R.C. model planes because they can save an enormous amount of money by using model planes, and besides that a pilot does not have to be in the plane when shooting those amazing crash scenes. (23) R.C. planes and technologies have also been adopted by the aerospace industries and the military for experimental flights so as not to endanger anyone, and for the gathering of information in conflict situations.

RESTATEMENT

SUPPORTING DETAILS

CONCLUDING REMARKS

(24) **Flying Radio Control planes** can be an *exciting* and *education* experience. (25) Even though many wives would tell you these things are just another toy for grown men, I would have to disagree. (25) I believe anyone who has had that dream of learning to fly would really enjoy flying a radio controlled airplane.

Essay by Edward P. Kruger

OPENING REMARKS   (1) Tired of school, exams, study, long cold winters, short days, cars not starting? (2) Take a trip with me to the exotic islands of *Cozumel* and

THESIS STATEMENT   *Grand Caymen* for my **underwater fantasy** come true.

TOPIC SENTENCE   (3) The first stop on my **dream dive** was the island of *Cozumel*. (4) After a brief meeting, my diving partner Danny and I geared up and entered the water from shore. (5) After swimming approximately fifty to seventy five feet underwater, pausing to enjoy a few small boats that were sunk to provide coral reefs for fish to live and eat, we came upon our

SUPPORTING DETAILS   destination. (6) There, at a depth of forty two feet, was a statue approximately fifteen to twenty feet high nestled in the sand. (7) It was of a woman, possibly some sort of Mayan Priestess whose arms were extended outward as if to accept the sun's rays penetrating the water from above. (8) We swam around, pausing for pictures with our underwater friend. (9) Noticing my air was low, we decided to head back to shore where we could discuss the wonders we just experienced.

TOPIC SENTENCE   (10) Our **second dive stop** was the island of *Grand Caymen*. (11) We boarded a dive boat and headed about one quarter to one half mile out from shore. (12) After a brief meeting, Danny and I geared up and entered the water. (13) Breaking the surface, I noticed the wreck that was our destination. (14) Descending down the anchor line approximately sixty five to seventy feet was a boat used to transport food to the island. (15) It came to rest on its side, cracking in half after a storm that had hit some twelve years earlier. (16) Nothing could have prepared me for what

SUPPORTING DETAILS   I was about to see. (17) Exhilarating was the only way to describe the site that lay before me. (18) Plants surrounded and covered the boat. (19) Exotic fish such as Parrot, Trumpet, and even the occasional Moray eel all call this underwater condominium home. (20) All this against a backdrop of spiny lobsters that call the richly colored blue and green coral their home. (21) Our air supply low, Danny and I returned to the boat,

taking only pictures for our friends back home to enjoy.

RESTATEMENT   (22) Nothing could have prepared me for the passionate tropical

breezes or the rich azure waters of Cozumel and Grand Caymen in the

CONCLUDING   Caribbean. (23) So, if you ever want to try something completely new,
REMARKS

try scuba diving. (24) Better yet, try scuba diving in the Caribbean.

6.2 Postwriting

These two essays were turned in by the students after they had proofread their essays. **Postwriting** is the last step in the writing process and an important one. Much like announcers of postgame show analyze the just-completed game, so writers analyze their rough drafts before writing the final copies. It is a much more specific process, though, than simply reading the essay over and over until the writer has a migraine.

Postwriting consists of both *editing* and *revising*: editing concerns grammar and revising concerns organization. The writer needs to look at the rough draft very carefully to be sure it not only says what the writer wants it to say, but also that it says it all in the most effective way. Use the following questions to help you analyze your rough draft.

Editing Questions:
(Chapters 7 - 15)

1) Are all the words spelled correctly?
2) Are the first words of sentences capitalized?
3) Is the vocabulary college level?
4) Are all the sentences punctuated correctly?
5) Are the commas correctly used?
6) Is there a variety of sentences?
7) Are there any sentences that should be joined for easier reading?
8) Are the pronouns consistent?
9) Do all the subjects agree with their verbs in number?
10) Are the verb tenses consistent?

Revising Questions:
(Chapters 1 - 6)

1) Is the opening interesting?
2) Is the thesis clearly stated?
3) Are the topic sentences clear?
4) Is each body paragraph complete?
5) Are the details specific enough?
6) Are there enough details?
7) Are there enough transitions?
8) Is the restatement clearly stated?
9) Do the last sentences leave the reader thinking about the subject?
10) Is the essay logically organized and interesting?

Once you are sure your essay says exactly what you want it to say in the best possible way, then you need to copy it over carefully. Your plan has now become an essay — one you can be proud to have written.

LEVELS ONE AND TWO EXERCISE

Read the following essay carefully and answer the questions on the lines provided.

(1) Suppose you are offered a better job with high wages and good benefits, and all you have to do is fill out the job application. (2) For most of us, the opportunity is easily taken, but for those who cannot read or write, the opportunity is lost. (3) Functional illiterates suffer two distinct disadvantages in our society: their job opportunities are limited and their ability to utilize modern conveniences is limited.

(4) In terms of job opportunities, the functional illiterate members of society are at a definite disadvantage. (5) First, they cannot read the want ads of a newspaper or local pennysaver to find out what jobs are available, nor can they read help wanted signs posted in business windows. (6) Thus, they are limited to word of mouth notification of job opportunities. (7) Second, once they determine where a job opening exists, they must be able to reach their destination by either boarding the correct bus or following appropriate street signs since driving a car is out of the question because of the written exam needed to obtain a license. (8) Assuming they do reach the place of employment, their third obstacle is filling out the job application should one be required. (9) Even the blank marked name would be incomprehensible. (10) Fourth, the job itself must require no reading or writing. (11) There are few jobs which do not require some of both. (12) For example, a restaurant waiter or waitress must be able to read the menu and then write down orders. (13) Consequently, functional illiterates are generally limited to low paying, unskilled jobs such as janitor or dish washer.

(14) The second disadvantage encountered by those who cannot read or write is the limited ability to use many modern conveniences. (15) The inability to drive and the difficulty of reading bus routes have already been mentioned. (16) Thus, mobility is greatly decreased for functional illiterates. (17) Two other modern conveniences outside the scope of the functionally illiterate are the checkbook and the credit card; since the former requires the ability to write the name of the payee and to write the amount of the check in words, the functionally illiterate cannot use a checkbook. (18) The credit card requires an application and unless they can find someone else to fill out such an application, the functionally illiterate cannot use the credit card either. (19) Furthermore, these people are also excluded from using the Automated Teller Machines which require appropriate responses to "written" questions. (20) Consequently, these people are limited to making cash purchases, assuming they can understand the price tags and remit the correct amount of cash. (21) Finally, it's also obvious that the functionally illiterate cannot obtain information from newspapers, magazines, or even swap sheets. (22) Their only source of information is either the television or the radio.

(23) Thus, the disadvantages of being unable to read or write are limited job opportunities and limited use of modern conveniences. (24) The functionally illiterate need, not our pity, but our help in becoming fully participating and productive members of our society. (25) Without our help, they are doomed to their own ignorance and poverty.

Questions

_____ 1. Which sentence contains the thesis statement?

_____ 2. How many aspects of the subject are in the thesis statement?

_____ 3. Which sentence(s) contains the opening remark?

_____ 4. Which sentence contains the first topic sentence?

_____ 5. Which sentence contains the second topic sentence?

_____ 6. Which sentence contains the restatement of the thesis?

_____ 7. Which sentence(s) contains the concluding remark?

_____ 8. Name one of the transitions used in the first body paragraph.

_____ 9. Name one of the transitions used in the second body paragraph.

_____ 10. Name the transition in the restatement of the thesis.

6.3 WRITING WORKSHOP — LEVELS ONE AND TWO

Definition: A writing workshop allows each student to work at his or her own pace in class and receive a grade for the finished paragraph or essay. The workshop will last several class periods to enable students to receive individual help from the instructor. Students requiring extra help may see the instructor during his or her office hours.

STEPS:

☞ **One:** Write a paragraph (LEVEL ONE) or essay (LEVEL TWO) on any subject of your choice after completing the prewriting for each paragraph or essay.

☞ **Two:** Bring the rough draft to the instructor for suggestions and corrections.

☞ **Three:** Rewrite the rough draft making all corrections necessary.

☞ **Four:** Bring the finished copy to the instructor for a grade.

☞ **Five:** Begin another paragraph or essay on a different subject of your choice and repeat the process.

POLICIES:

1. Students should maintain a quiet atmosphere.

2. All paragraphs or essays are written in class.

3. Each student works on **one** essay at a time. MULTIPLE ESSAYS WILL NOT BE EVALUATED. Bring only one at a time to the instructor.

4. Each student must complete a minimum of five (5) paragraphs or essays during the workshop session. Students may write up to seven (7) paragraphs or essays for extra credit.

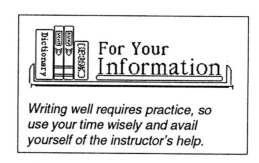

For Your
Information

Writing well requires practice, so use your time wisely and avail yourself of the instructor's help.

6.4 TOPIC CHOICES (suggestions only)

1. Explain one or two reasons you feel your high school did or did not prepare you for college level work.
2. Explain one or two reasons everyone should vote.
3. Describe one or two health problems you feel require national attention.
4. Describe one or two differences between your high school and college.
5. Explain two or three of the results of a college education.

6. Discuss two or three reasons you have chosen your particular career field.
7. Explain two or three reasons writing well is important in every day life.
8. Discuss the advantages or disadvantages of waiting several years before attending college.
9. Describe two or three attributes you feel students need to be successful in school.
10. Discuss two or three reasons professional athletes do or do not deserve million dollar salaries.

11. Compare two musical groups to show which one is better.
12. Discuss two or three ways parents can improve communication with their children.
13. Describe two or three people who have had a positive influence on your life.
14. Describe two or three similarities or differences between your childhood and your parents' childhood.
15. Explain two or three advantages of any hobby you may have.

16. Explain two or three reasons everyone should learn about computers.
17. Discuss two or three ways technology has changed your life.
18. Discuss two or three reasons you feel labor unions are effective or ineffective.
19. Describe two or three ways a consumer can protect himself or herself when making major purchases.
20. Describe one or two life values you consider important (e.g., honesty, discipline, etc.).

21. Discuss two or three reasons you feel preserving nature is important.
22. Discuss two or three reasons you feel college athletes should or should not have to maintain a certain academic standard to participate in sports.
23. Explain one or two causes of student failure in college.
24. Explain two or three reasons you feel credit cards are assets or liabilities.
25. Explain two or three causes of elderly abuse.

26. Explain one or two reasons you feel the nuclear family is on the rise or on the decline.
27. Describe one or two ways the role of women in society has changed.
28. Describe one or two examples of obnoxious television commercials.
29. Describe one or two examples of prejudice you or someone you know may have encountered.
30. Explain one or two ways to help the homeless in the United States.

31. Describe one or two positive or negative effects playing team sports may have on an individual player.

32. Explain one or two reasons the plans for a space station should or should not move forward.

33. Explain one or two ways an individual can overcome stress.

34. Discuss two or three reasons the private lives of presidential candidates should or should not be examined.

35. Discuss one or two ways to improve trade relations between Japan and the United States.

36. Explain two or three primary steps an individual can take to get a better job.

37. Explain one or two ways to protect children from violence on television.

38. Discuss one or two reasons everyone should or should not be required to take a foreign language.

39. Explain two or three advantages or disadvantages of personal computers.

40. Explain one or two results of divorce on children.

41. Explain one or two reasons you feel Congress is effective or ineffective in making decisions.

42. Explain one or two ways to better health.

43. Discuss one or two effects of caring for an elderly relative at home.

44. Discuss one or two results of volunteering in community projects.

45. Describe one or two incidents that changed your life.

46. Describe two or three examples of excellent television programming for children.

47. Explain one or two reasons the school year should or should not be extended to include the summer months.

48. Describe two or three people you feel are national heroes.

49. Discuss two or three suggestions for improving your school's curricula.

50. Explain one or two reasons the immigration laws of the United States should or should not be changed.

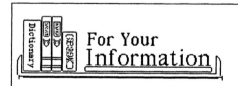

For Your
Information

If you have access to a computer or word processor, you may find that writing is easier. Give it a try.

Chapter Seven

PARTS OF SPEECH

7.1 Nouns

7.2 Verbs

7.3 Pronouns

7.4 Modifiers

      Adverbs
      Adjectives
      Prepositional Phrases

KEY TERMS

Adjectives .... describe nouns

Adverbs .... describe verbs, adjectives or other adverbs

Modifiers .... describe nouns, pronouns, or verbs

Nouns .... name persons, places, things, or ideas

Prepositional Phrases .... may be either adverbs or adjectives

Pronouns .... take the place of nouns

Verbs .... show action or link one part of a sentence to another part

The loother thurly naxated the hooms by the slan pirt.

No, this isn't a good typist on a humid day, but it is a nonsense sentence. Because we are accustomed to hearing English spoken most of our lives, we can name the various parts of this sentence.

The loother thurly naxated the hooms by the slan pirt.
adj   noun   adverb   verb   adj   noun   prep adj adj noun

We can tell that **loother** is a noun because we're accustomed to seeing or hearing the word **the** before a noun. **Thurly** has the "ly" ending usually found on adverbs. **Naxated** has an "ed" ending usually found on verbs showing past tense. **Hooms** has a plural form as well as the word **the** before it making it a noun. **By** is a preposition and since most prepositional phrases end with noun, **pirt** must be a noun. The words **the** and **slan** become adjectives describing the noun **pirt**. In other words, we can usually determine what part of speech a word is by its clues. It helps to understand the categories or parts of speech a word may play in a sentence.

7.1 NOUNS

Definition: A noun names a person, place, thing, or idea. It may be specific such as *John Smith, Fort Lauderdale, robin, democracy*, or it may be general such as *boy, forest, bird, proposal*.

Characteristics: A noun may be made plural by adding an "s" or "es" such as boys, forests, birds, marshes. It may also be introduced by an article such as "a," "an," "the" — *the boy, a forest, an apple*. Occasionally, it may have an "ing" ending such as *eating, thinking, shopping*. These may look like verbs, but without a helping word to make them verbs, they are nouns.

Function in a sentence: A noun may be the subject of the sentence or an object. If it is the subject, it will have a verb with it. There may be more than one noun functioning as the subject in a sentence. The subject is often first in the sentence, but it may be anywhere.

Examples:

John Smith was married to **Pocahontas**.
　　subject　　　　　　　　　　　object

Russia is working toward **democracy**.
subject　　　　　　　　　　object

The **explanation** was confusing.
　　subject

The **bombing** of **Iraq** drove **Hussein** out of **Kuwait**.
　　subject　　　object　　　object　　　　object

Eating correctly is one **way** to stay healthy.
subject   object

Men and **women** have a difficult **time** communicating their **feelings**.
subject   subject   object   object

Titles of **books** are often misleading.
subject   object

There are few **people** capable of **understanding** Hawking's **theory** of **time**.
                 subject   object   object   object

Prejudice is a **disease**.
 subject   object

Here are the **answers** to life's **problems**.
                  subject   object

7.2 VERBS

Definition: A verb shows action or links one part of a sentence to another part of the sentence.

Characteristics: A verb shows time — past (by adding "d" or "ed"), present, future (by adding will or shall). Some tenses require both the main verb and one or more helping (auxiliary) verbs. Some verbs form their tenses irregularly by altering the word itself.

Function in a sentence: The verb (with all the helping verbs) becomes the **predicate** of the sentence and shows the activity of the subject. It may be anywhere in the sentence, though it is usually after the subject. The verb may also link one part of the sentence to another part of the sentence; these verbs are called linking verbs (examples of linking verbs: *am, are, is, was, were,* HAS, HAD, HAVE *seem, feel, grow*). There may be more than one verb in a sentence. Usually verbs with the word "to" in front of them are not verbs in the sentence.

Examples:

Mr. Smith **is going** to Washington.
            predicate (verb)

Weekends **were made** for mowing.
            predicate (verb)

The tourists **followed** their guide to the bottom of the page.
                predicate (verb)

Russia **is** in a state of radical change and **needs** the world's help.
     predicate (verb)   predicate (verb)

Adventure films **are** too violent for young children.
              predicate (verb)

Freddy **finished** his homework and **went** to his choir meeting.
     predicate (verb)   predicate (verb)

Feeding the cat, taking out the trash, and eating breakfast **are** morning chores.
                                       predicate (verb)

Studying well **requires** practice and determination.
          predicate (verb)

Most Americans **have had** a high school education.
        predicate (verb)

7.3 PRONOUNS

Definition: Pronouns are words that replace nouns. Without them, we would be doomed to the following kind of writing:

> **Harry** wanted to be a writer, so **Harry** wrote day and night. **Harry** planned to finish **Harry's** first novel in less than a week. **Harry** thought **Harry** could do it without any problem. **Harry** wrote until **Harry's** hand cramped up. After three days, **Harry** decided **Harry** better get a real job.

By replacing some of the nouns with pronouns, this passage becomes much easier to read and far less boring.

> **Harry** wanted to be a writer, so **he** wrote day and night. **He** planned to finish **his** first novel in less than a week. **Harry** thought **he** could do it without any problem. **He** wrote until **his** hand cramped up. After three days, **he** decided he better get a real job.

Characteristics: Two of the most common types of pronouns are *personal pronouns* and *indefinite pronouns* (indefinite pronouns usually end in "one" or "body" and do not refer to a specific person). (See Chapter Twelve)

Function in a sentence: A pronoun may be the subject , the object in a sentence, or may show possession. Possessive pronouns do not need an apostrophe; they do, however, need a "noun" to possess. There may be more than one subject or object in a sentence, and there may be more than one possession in a sentence.

The following chart shows the **personal pronouns** and three of their functions in a sentence.

Subject Pronouns	Object Pronouns	Possessive Pronouns
I	me	my, mine
you	you	your, yours
he	him	his
she	her	her, hers
it	it	its
we	us	our, ours
they	them	their, theirs

Examples:

I will give **you** a new way of looking at the world.
subject   object

They left **their** hearts in San Diego.
subject   possessive (the noun "possessed" is "hearts")

We always have to wait for **them** to get ready.
subject   object

It is always a challenge to find answers to new questions.
subject

You will find **us** prepared to learn.
subject   object

Get the lead out.
(**You** is understood to be the subject.
"You" is the only pronoun that can be implied.)

Between **you** and **me**, the world is a small place.
        object   object

He wanted **us** to go with **him** to the mud-wrestling tournament.
subject   object   object

Nobody likes Harry's dog because of **its** mean bark.
subject (indefinite pronoun)   possession (the noun possessed is "bark")

We need **someone** shorter for the role of Lady Macbeth.
subject   object (indefinite pronoun)

7.4 MODIFIERS

Definition: Modifiers are words that describe something in the sentence. Suppose someone told you that you could have a million dollars simply by going out to a truck in the parking lot and getting the suitcase with the money. You look out in the parking lot and see at least fifty trucks. What you need is more description to find the right truck.

> **The extremely rusty, red pick-up** truck **with two broken headlights** has a million dollars **in the front seat**.

All the added information will make it easier for you to pick up your money!

Characteristics: There are three basic types of modifiers: **adjectives, adverbs** and **prepositional phrases**.

Function in a sentence: Modifiers describe subjects or predicates by adding more information. A sentence may contain any number of modifiers. Generally, the modifier is placed near the word it is describing to avoid any confusion on the reader's part. A modifier is considered "misplaced" when it is too far away from the word it describes (ex: *George* stood near the piano **with a cane**.)

❏ **Adjectives**

Definition: An adjective describes a noun.

Characteristics: The adjective may come before the noun, after the noun and after a linking verb. Articles such as **a, an** and **the** are also considered adjectives. There may be any number of adjectives in a sentence.

Examples:

An **excellent** teacher can explain a **difficult** concept.
　　adjective　　　　　　　　　　adjective

The **happy** homemaker is a stereotype.
　　adjective

The **dilapidated** house had **broken** windows, **torn** shutters, and **loose** wires.
　　adjective　　　　　adjective　　　　adjective　　　　adjective

Gary Cooper was **tall, elegant, handsome** and **charming**.
　　　　　adjective adjective　adjective　　adjective

Floods take a **heavy** toll on **weary** homeowners.
　　　　　adjective　　　　adjective

❏ **Adverbs**

Definition: An adverb may describe a verb, an adjective or another adverb.

Characteristics: The adverb may come before or after the verb. It usually comes before an adjective or another adverb. Adverbs also show frequency (**often, seldom**) and quantity (**too**). Some adverbs end in "ly." There may be any number of adverbs in a sentence.

Examples:

A good speaker *speaks* **slowly** and *enunciates* **properly**.
　　　　　　predicate adverb　　　predicate　adverb

Calculus is an **extremely** *difficult* subject to master.
　　　　　　adverb　　adjective

Quickly, the predator *snatched* his prey.
adverb　　　　　　predicate

An **exceptionally** intelligent student will **often** do **very well**.
　adverb　　adjective　　　　　adverb　adverb adverb

The adverb can **never** modify a noun.
　　　　　　adverb

⊠ **Prepositional Phrases**

Definition: A prepositional phrase is a group of words consisting of a preposition (*of, in, by, behind, near, to, on*) and a noun or pronoun. Between the preposition and the noun or pronoun may be any number of adverbs and/or adjectives.

Characteristics: Prepositional phrases may be anywhere in a sentence and give added information about the subject or the predicate. They are not considered part of the subject, however.

Examples:

Harry searched <u>for the cat</u> <u>in the trash</u>, <u>in the attic</u>, <u>on the roof</u>, and <u>behind the barn</u>.
　　　　　　prep.　　　prep.　　　prep.　　　prep.　　　　prep.

<u>After the war</u>, many men were scarred <u>for life</u> <u>by the violence</u>.
prep.　　　　　　　　　　　　　　　prep.　　prep.

One <u>of the ways</u> to promote racial harmony is to learn <u>about different cultures</u>.
　　prep.　　　　　　　　　　　　　　　　　　prep.

Each <u>of us</u> must become aware <u>of our similarities</u> <u>to one another</u>.
prep.   prep.   prep.

He applied <u>for a job</u> <u>at the grocery store</u>, <u>at the gas station</u> and <u>at the cleaners</u>.
prep.   prep.   prep.   prep.

(The last example could also be written this way: He applied <u>for a job</u> <u>at the grocery store,</u> <u>the gas station</u> and <u>the cleaners</u>. **Grocery store, gas station** and **cleaners** all become objects of the preposition "at.")

The **adjective, adverb** and **prepositional phrase** all add more information to the sentence to make the sentence more specific. Life without them would be very dull.

These primary parts of speech make our sentences interesting, intelligent and understandable. So, a sentence is only as good as its parts. When choosing your **nouns, verbs, indefinite pronouns, adjectives, adverbs** and **prepositional phrase ,** choose wisely and be specific. One of the joys — and terrors — of English is the number of ways to say the same thing. One way is not necessarily "better" than another way, although sometimes subtle word changes can change an idea. Take a look at the examples below and decide for yourself which is more effective. Remember that it's not only what you say, but how effectively you say it.

Violence is bad.
Violence on television is bad.
Violence on television should be regulated by the federal government.
Violence on television has a negative influence on young children.

NOTE: A **simple sentence** must contain a subject and a verb (predicate). Every example sentence in this chapter is a simple sentence. A simple sentence is not defined by length and may contain any number of subjects and verbs. (See Chapter Eight, Independent Clause, page 67)

Example:
Harry, *Bill* and *Joe* **ate** a big breakfast, **packed** their van, and **left** for their cabin.
subj   subj   subj verb   verb   verb

A formula for a simple sentence is **S + V.**

LEVEL ONE EXERCISE:

Number from one to fifty on a separate sheet of paper and name the part of speech of each of the underlined words.

1. The <u>tall</u> <u>man</u> <u>at the door</u> <u>had</u> a <u>bright</u> <u>red</u> <u>moustache</u> and <u>extremely</u> <u>long</u> <u>hair</u>.
       1   2   3   4   5   6   7   8   9 10

2. <u>Everyone</u> <u>went</u> <u>to the party</u> and <u>had</u> a <u>wonderful</u> <u>time</u>.
       11   12   13   14   15   16

3. <u>Harry's</u> <u>mother</u> <u>grounded</u> <u>him</u> <u>for two weeks</u>.
       17   18   19   20   21

4. The <u>war</u> <u>in the Gulf</u> <u>focused</u> our <u>attention</u> <u>on the problems</u> <u>in the Middle East</u>.
       22   23   24   25   26   27

5. <u>You</u> <u>left</u> <u>your</u> <u>book</u> <u>on the table</u> <u>near the door</u>.
     28 29 30 31   32   33

6. The <u>woman</u> <u>with blue hair</u> <u>wears</u> an <u>extraordinarily</u> <u>long</u> <u>earring</u> <u>in one ear</u>.
         34   35   36   37   38 39   40

7. <u>John</u> and <u>I</u> <u>are going</u> <u>to the concert</u> <u>reluctantly</u>.
     41   42   43   44   45

8. The <u>Romans</u> <u>had</u> an <u>extremely</u> <u>violent</u> <u>nature</u>.
       46   47   48   49   50

LEVEL TWO EXERCISE:

Follow the directions for each of the sentences below.

1. Write a simple sentence using a pronoun as a subject.

2. Write a simple sentence using an "ing" word as a subject.

3. Write a simple sentence using two prepositional phrases.

4. Write a simple sentence containing two adverbs.

5. Write a simple sentence containing three adjectives.

6. Write a simple sentence containing two nouns as subjects.

7. Write a simple sentence containing two different verbs as predicates.

8. Write a simple sentence containing two pronouns as objects.

9. Write a simple sentence containing one noun and one pronoun as subjects.

10. Write a simple sentence containing all of the parts of speech.

Chapter Eight

Coordination

Coordination and Subordination (Chapter Nine) are writing methods. They help to show relationships between ideas. To understand and use these two techniques well, you must first know the terms used in this chapter and the next chapter. Memorize them.

8.1 Clause

8.2 Independent Clause

8.3 Coordination and Coordinating Conjunctions

8.4 Conjunctive Adverbs

Key Terms

Clause .... group of words containing a subject and a verb

Conjunctive Adverb .... an adverb that can join two sentences

Coordinating Conjunction .... a word that joins two complete sentences

Coordination .... joining two complete and equal sentences

Independent Clause .... group of words containing a subject and a verb; expresses a complete idea

8.1 The Clause

Definition: The **Clause** is a group of words containing a subject and a verb.

Examples:

> 1) The family **car** *is* five years old.
>   subj verb

> 2) ...because **I** *subscribe* to several magazines...
>   subj verb

> 3) **Sam** *makes* the best coffee.
>   subj verb

(Notice that numbers 1 and 3 are complete sentences and can stand alone. But number 2, although it is a clause with a subject and a verb, is not a sentence. More about this in Chapter 9.)

LEVELS ONE AND TWO EXERCISE 8.1

Mark "yes" if the item is a clause. Mark "no" if the item is not a clause.

_____1) ...over the hills and through the trees...

_____2) ...when Professor Ample passes the vending machines...

_____3) ...my printer is malfunctioning again...

_____4) ...although Fred scored 90 on the test...

_____5) ...my cat, Hairball, is very good at ping pong...

_____6) ...the singers Peter, Paul, and Mary...

_____7) ...at the moment...

_____8) ...when Sasha finished her research paper...

_____9) ...are pineapples and pine cones related...

_____10) ...Jones built a raft and sailed away...

8.2 The Independent Clause

Definition: The **independent clause** is one that expresses a complete idea.
It is a sentence, and it can stand alone.

Examples:

      1) **Studying** *is* hard work.
          subj   verb

      2) **Professor Cloudy** *has visited* Europe several times.
          subj   verb

      3) These days **one** *has* to ask for ice water in a restaurant.
                subj verb

LEVELS ONE AND TWO EXERCISE 8.2

Mark "yes" if the item is an independent clause. Mark "no" if the item is not
an independent clause.

_____1) ...as soon as you finish your complaining...

_____2) ...the radio telescope picks up radio waves from the stars...

_____3) ...I hate rainy days...

_____4) ...since you seem to have all the answers...

_____5) ...give me back my Raggedy Ann doll...

_____6) ...on the refrigerator and under the cigar box...

_____7) ...Professor Daft wears mismatched sneakers...

_____8) ...Raj comes from India...

_____9) ...four fish heads and three dozen pinto beans...

_____10) ...verbs are words that express action or condition...

8.3 Coordination

Definition: Join two independent clauses (2 complete ideas) with a comma and a coordinating conjunction (a short connector).

,AND   ,BUT   ,SO   ,OR
,NOR   ,FOR   ,YET

NOTE: The coordinating conjunction (short connector) indicates that two ideas are of equal value. The two ideas are coordinated or balanced.

COORDINATING CONJUNCTIONS OR SHORT CONNECTORS INDICATE RELATIONSHIPS BETWEEN IDEAS

1) **,AND** indicates ADDITION
    I studied hard ,AND I passed with an "A".
(One complete idea is merely added to another of equal importance.

2) **,BUT** indicates CONTRAST
    Senator Stalwart asked for more funds, BUT he did not receive additional money.
(The second complete idea is in contrast with the first one.)

3) **,SO** indicates CAUSE & EFFECT (or result)
    Luciano twisted his knee playing tennis, SO he could not dig up the flower bed.
(The situation in the second independent clause is the result of what happened in the first.)

4) **,OR** indicates CHOICE
    I must have a pay increase, OR I will look elsewhere for work.
(Somebody will choose to quit if denied a raise.)

5) **,NOR** indicates NEITHER ONE
    Jones is not trustworthy, NOR is he competent.
(Not one nor the other. Both ideas of equal importance.)

6) **,FOR** indicates BECAUSE
    Jade is expensive in jewelry and ornaments, FOR it is extremely hard and difficult to carve.
(One clause is cause; the other is effect. The ideas are balanced with a short connector.)

7) **,YET** indicates CONTRAST

> Mr. Faulty has known about the bad plumbing for over a year, YET he has done nothing about it.

(If you can use "but" accurately, you can also use "yet" in the same way. Try it for variety. "Yet" and "but" give us an idea in the second clause that is in contrast to what we expect after reading the first clause.)

REMINDER: Coordinate and balance ideas

More Examples:

1) I registered for college, AND I start classes in January.
2) An outboard motor boat is a lot of fun, BUT it makes too much noise.
3) Professor Idle was ten minutes late for class, SO the students left in a great mood.
4) You can have the spaghetti with marinara sauce, OR you can have the grilled fish.
5) Joe Clown is not interested in biology, NOR is he interested in math.
6) Whale populations are now growing, FOR hunting has been banned.
7) Shakespeare is a bit difficult to read, YET he can be extremely interesting.

REMINDER: When you connect two independent clauses with a coordinating conjunction, DON'T FORGET THE COMMA THAT GOES WITH IT, as in the many examples above.

VARY THE LENGTH OF YOUR SENTENCE. A series of short sentences can present a very choppy effect. If you think about it, you will find that many of your ideas are related to each other, and the relationships can be shown with coordinating conjunctions. (We will also call them short connectors in this chapter.)

UNCOORDINATED WRITING:

> My neighbor has an aboveground swimming pool. Her five children use it every day in the summer. The children make an incredible amount of noise. It is not reasonable to expect them to be quiet. I need a peaceful place to study. I must go to the town library. Study in my room is impossible. The swimming pool full of kids is just outside my window. I know kids must play. I sometimes wish they would all go someplace else.

This is dull. Notice the start-and-stop choppiness. Avoid this effect with the correct use of the short connectors, as in the sample on the next page.

COORDINATED WRITING:

> My neighbor has an aboveground swimming pool, AND her five children use it every day in the summer. The children make an incredible amount of noise, AND it is not reasonable to expect them to be quiet. BUT I need a peaceful place to study, SO I must go to the town library. Study in my room is impossible, FOR the swimming pool full of kids is just outside my window. I know kids must play, YET I sometimes wish they would all go someplace else.

Coordinated writing has a more "adult" sound to it because the equally important independent clauses are balanced against one another with conjunctions. This is one kind of writing a college student should be able to do.

Giant Ampersand Anyone?

&

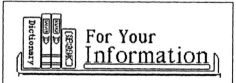

For Your Information

In formal college writing, avoid using the ampersand; write out the word "and."

LEVEL ONE EXERCISE 8.3

Fill in the appropriate coordinating conjunction (*and, but, so, or, for, nor, yet*) which indicates the relationship between the two independent clauses:

1) Mr. Faulty has weak knees, _____ his eyesight is poor.
                    [ADDITION]

2) The marina was closed, _____ we sneaked in anyway.
                    [CONTRAST]

3) John Q. Student forgot to study, _____ he failed.
                    [CAUSE AND EFFECT]

4) I will go to college, _____ I will enter the military.
                    [CHOICE]

5) Luciano cut his math class, _____ he forgot his text.
                    [BECAUSE]

6) I won't promise, _____ will I pay.
                    [NEITHER ONE]

7) Ms. Placid loves sweets, _____ she won't eat chocolate.
                    [CONTRAST]

8) You should not stare, _____ should you point.
                    [NEITHER ONE]

9) The transmission went to pieces, _____ I stopped the car.
                    [CAUSE & EFFECT]

10) I will use half-and-half, _____ I won't use cream.
                    [CONTRAST]

LEVEL TWO EXERCISE 8.3

Fill in the appropriate coordinating conjunction (*and, but, so, or, for, nor, yet*) which indicates the relationship between the two independent clauses:

1) Ali Akbar enjoys living in the United States, _____ he must return to Iran very soon.

[CONTRAST]

2) Betty Crackers baked three cakes for the Lardo Society, _____ she sent them by priority mail.   [ADDITION]

3) Foreign automobiles are noted for their reliability, _____ they can be much more expensive than American cars.   [CONTRAST]

4) It was difficult to drive from the downtown area out to the airport, _____ the country funded a brand new expressway.   [CAUSE & EFFECT]

5) You can buy a computer right now, _____ you can wait six months and take advantage of the newest developments.   [CHOICE]

6) Professor Bustling is extremely difficult to talk to, _____ he is constantly in a hurry.

[BECAUSE]

7) Oregon does not wish to destroy its forest, _____ does the state wish to eliminate thousands of lumber industry jobs.   [NEITHER ONE]

8) The movie *Jurassic Park* is a favorite among young and old, _____ what could be more fascinating than dinosaurs?   [BECAUSE]

9) The President's nomination for Attorney General was not accepted by Congress, _____ the search for a highly qualified candidate began again.
[CAUSE & EFFECT]

10) You must pay your taxes, _____ you are in for a surprise from the IRS.
[CHOICE]

8.4 CONJUNCTIVE ADVERBS [long connectors]

Join two independent clauses (2 complete ideas) with a semi-colon, a conjunctive adverb + a comma.

Example:

Fred received a huge electric shock**; however,** he will live.
subj verb   ; long connector, subj verb

If you can use the short connectors discussed in this chapter (the coordinating conjunctions), then certainly you can use the long connectors.

There are good reasons to do so:

> For one thing, the long connectors are more *emphatic* in showing the relationship between two independent clauses.
> For another, they are *classy*, often used by knowledgeable writers.
> Also, the long connectors are a bit more *formal*, and can give your writing a greater sense of credibility, or authority.

AMONG THE MANY LONG CONNECTORS ARE:

;however,	indicates CONTRAST just like ,BUT
;therefore,	indicates CAUSE & EFFECT just like ,SO
;consequently,	indicates CAUSE & EFFECT just like ,SO
;furthermore,	indicates ADDITION just like ,AND
;nevertheless,	indicates CONTRAST just like ,BUT
;in addition,	indicates ADDITION just like ,AND
;as a result,	indicates CAUSE & EFFECT just like ,SO

Notice that the long connectors given above each have a semi-colon before and a comma after. Again, this is standard punctuation when they are used to connect two independent clauses.

1) **;HOWEVER,** indicates CONTRAST
   The board members met for three hours; HOWEVER, they accomplished very little.
(The idea in the second independent clause is in contrast to what might be expected from the first.)

2) **;THEREFORE,** indicates CAUSE & EFFECT
   Our computer is down; THEREFORE, we are behind in our work.
(The first clause gives the cause, and the second gives the effect.)

3) **;CONSEQUENTLY,** indicates CAUSE & EFFECT

My grades are too low; CONSEQUENTLY, the Nursing Department has asked me to withdraw.

(Low grades are the cause; withdrawal is the effect or result.)

4) **;FURTHERMORE,** indicates ADDITION

Oil spills are deadly to the environment; FURTHERMORE, they are enormously expensive to clean up.

(One idea is emphatically added to another.)

5) **;NEVERTHELESS,** indicates CONTRAST

Mountain climbing can be life-threatening; NEVERTHELESS, Professor Bustling climbs every summer.

(One idea is in contrast with the other.)

6) **;IN ADDITION,** indicates ADDITION

My dentist said I had several cavities; IN ADDITION, he said I needed a root canal!

(The second idea is added to the first with greater emphasis than one gets with "and.")

7) **;AS A RESULT,** indicates CAUSE & EFFECT

He continued to ignore my warnings about driving too fast; AS A RESULT, he finally had a terrible accident.

(You can use "so" in this sentence instead of the long connector, but if you do, the sentence will sound weaker.)

Compound (Coordinated) Sentence Formulas

It may be easier to remember how to construct a coordinated or compound sentence by remembering two simple formulas:

Subject + Verb, coordinating conjunction Subject + Verb.
Independent Clause   (and, but, or, etc.)   Independent Clause
S+V, cc S+V.

OR

Subject + Verb; Adverbial Conjunction, Subject + Verb.
Independent Clause   (however, therefore, etc.)   Independent Clause
S+V; ac, S+V.

LEVEL ONE EXERCISE 8.4

Insert one of the following long connectors into the space provided: *;however,* —
;consequently, — *;furthermore,* — *;nevertheless,* — *;in addition,* — *;as a result,*

1) I went to see Professor Ample _____ he was not in his office.
[CONTRAST]

2) Computers were on sale for 40% off _____ I bought one.
[CAUSE & EFFECT]

3) Fish disappeared from the lake _____ swimming was prohibited.
[ADDITION]

4) A meteorite fell on Indiana _____ it killed a dog.
[ADDITION]

5) The eagle is a protected bird in the U. S. _____ Joe Clown
blasted one out of the sky with a shotgun.   [CONTRAST]

6) We went to sunny Hawaii for a week _____ it rained six days
out of seven.
[CONTRAST]

7) Mrs. Counterpane went on a crash diet _____ she lost several
pounds in a week.   [CAUSE & EFFECT]

8) Mrs. Counterpane wished to celebrate _____ she ate several
pieces of cheese cake with whipped cream.   CAUSE & EFFECT]

9) The ancient Greeks lived in dangerous times _____ the average
adult died before the age of 40.   [ADDITION]

10) Some paleontologists believe dinosaurs had brightly colored skins
_____ nobody knows for sure.
[CONTRAST]

LEVEL TWO EXERCISE 8.4

Write a set of sentences using the long connectors given below. Make sure each sentence contains two independent clauses joined by the connector. Use correct punctuation.

1) [HOWEVER]

2) [AS A RESULT]

3) [THEREFORE]

4) [IN ADDITION]

5) [CONSEQUENTLY]

6) [NEVERTHELESS]

7) [FURTHERMORE]

CHAPTER 8 REVIEW EXERCISES

LEVEL ONE AND TWO 8.2 (clauses)

Mark "yes" if the item is a clause. Mark "no" if the item is not a clause.

_____ 1) ...in one side and out the other...

_____ 2) ...since you are going to see Professor Blur...

_____ 3) ...the Acheson, Topeka, and the Sante Fe...

_____ 4) ...the President is in his helicopter...

_____ 5) ...being the one thing I hate...

_____ 6) ...Joe Clown had him in a hammerlock...

_____ 7) ...up to the stoplight and to your left...

_____ 8) ...the Grand Coulee dam is the largest in the world...

_____ 9) ...stop that right this minute...

_____ 10) ...although my dentist was arrested...

LEVEL ONE 8.3 (coordinators)

Fill in the appropriate short connector (coordinating conjunction — *and, but, so, or, for, nor, yet*) which indicates the relationship between the two independent clauses.

1) He refused to attend the wedding, he refused to explain why.

2) He gave her a ruby, she wanted a diamond.

3) Hairball is a huge cat, he does not eat much.

4) Joe Clown was late again, we went on without him

5) Jones was sent to the bench, he sat there for the rest of the game.

LEVEL TWO 8.3 (coordinators)

Fill in the appropriate short connector (coordinating conjunction — *and, but, so, or, for, nor, yet*) which indicates the relationship between the two independent clauses.

1) "As the crow flies" means in a straight line, "to eat crow" means to admit that one was wrong.

2) Queen Elizabeth's formal crowns are priceless, they are all kept under heavy guard in the Tower of London.

3) Mr. Faulty is not interested in the newspaper, he does read the comic page.

4) The Bovine Committee wished to commemorate their previous chairman, they named a new ice cream after him.

5) Auntie Upp would not ride in the family car, carsickness was one of her recurring problems.

LEVEL ONE 8.4 (conjunctive adverbs)

Insert one of the following long connectors into the space provided: *;however, — ;therefore, — ;consequently, — ;furthermore, — ;nevertheless, — ;in addition, — ;as a result,*

1) Some people need eight hours of sleep _____ some people do not.

2) The American Cancer Society does a great deal of good _____ I contribute to it yearly.

3) Sasha is interested in photography _____ she does not own a camera.

4) The suspect was observed at the scene of the crime _____ he left his footprints in the snow.

5) Killer bees from Africa have been discovered in Texas _____ they are moving north year by year.

LEVEL TWO EXERCISE 8.4 (conjunctive adverbs)

Insert one of the following long connectors into the space provided: *;however, —
;consequently, —;furthermore, — ;nevertheless, — ;in addition, — ;as a result,*

1) The octopus may not look very appetizing _____ many

   Mediterranean peoples enjoy having it on the menu.

2) Grandfather Casanova is a vegetarian, a daily swimmer, and a womanizer

   _____ he says, he has lived to be 90.

3) The Lardo Society thought that installing a computer would reduce paper costs

   _____ to everyone's surprise, the use of paper skyrocketed.

4) Marie Antoinette promised to amend her life _____ the French

   revolutionaries separated her from her head.

5) My cat, Hairball, is a master in the fine art of ambushing ankles_____

   he is superb at playing deaf.

Chapter Nine

Subordination

9.1 Dependent Clause

9.2 Dependent Clauses and Subordinators

9.3 Dependent Clause and the Comma

9.4 Subordination and Subordinating Conjunctions

Key Terms

Dependent Clause......................... a group of words containing a subject and a verb;
does not express a complete thought

Subordinating Conjunction .... a word that joins two sentences by making one sentence
a dependent clause

Subordination .... combining two sentences by making one sentence
a dependent clause

9.1 The Dependent Clause

Definition: The **dependent clause** is one that expresses an incomplete idea.
Even though it is a group of words with a subject and a verb, it is not a sentence, for it cannot stand alone. It must be attached to an independent clause.

Examples:

> 1) When the athletes marched into the arena...
> 2) Because Sam is a fine cook...
> 3) If a car is driven roughly...

Each of these *dependent clauses* needs an attached **independent clause** to make sense:

> 1) *When the athletes marched into the arena,* **the spectators welcomed them with a roar.**
> 2) **We ate well on our camping trip** *because Sam is a fine cook.*
> 3) *If a car is driven roughly,* **it probably will not last long.**

(Notice that an independent clause can come before or after a dependent clause.)

LEVELS ONE AND TWO EXERCISE 8.3

Mark "D" if the item is a dependent clause. Mark "I" if the item is an independent clause.

_____1) ...although Professor Cash has plenty of money...

_____2) ...there are several chambers in the human heart...

_____3) ...Venus is the most brilliant planet in the sky...

_____4) ...since you went astray...

_____5) ...while Mr. Impulse was buying his lotto tickets...

_____6) ...whenever you yell at your children...

_____7) ...everybody seems interested in country music...

_____8) ...because Yellowstone National Park is crowded with thousands of visitors...

_____9) ...if you come to the Lardo Society picnic...

_____10) ...as soon as he got woozy...

9.2 Dependent Clauses and Subordinating Conjunctions

Definition: The **subordinating conjunction** is a connecting word that makes one idea less important than another. (We will see more about this in section 9.4)

Examples of subordinators:

after		whenever
as soon as		while
before		because
since		if
unless		when
who	which	that (These last three are relative pronouns.)

Note: Jake has graduated from college.
       subj   verb

This is an **independent clause** and can stand alone as a finished idea. However, place a subordinator in front of it and then it will need a completing idea; an independent clause must be added for a complete sentence.

Note: *As soon as* Jake has graduated from college...

The subordinator *"as soon as"* has made the original idea less important and unfinished. We must add an independent clause, or main idea, to get a complete sentence.

Note: *As soon as Jake has graduated from college*, **he will begin work in the family business.**

LEVEL ONE EXERCISE 9.2

In the space provided write in a subordinating conjunction that shows the relationship between the clauses. Follow the example in number 1.

1) We stopped chattering <u>after</u> the movie began.

2) _____ you finish your dinner, come with me.

3) I was in politics _____ you were born.

4) _____ he smashed his dad's car, he lost his privileges.

5) _____ you do not help, you can live somewhere else.

LEVEL TWO EXERCISE 9.2

In the space provided write in a subordinating conjunction that shows the relationship between the clauses. Follow the example in number 1.

1) <u>Even though</u> I had read a great deal of history, I never found out much about Alexander the Great.

2) Professor Cloudy did not hear the question _____ he was dozing.

3) _____ you want to put some zip on your steak, add a little Worcestershire sauce.

4) _____ you enjoy sounding like an idiot, you had better learn something about feminism.

5) _____ Senator Stalwart was out of the chamber, somebody removed all the papers from his desk.

9.3 Dependent Clauses and the Comma

When a **dependent clause** introduces or comes before an independent clause, it is followed by a comma (just as in this sentence).

Examples:

1) *Even though my dog looks ferocious,* [comma] **he is really very gentle.**
2) *If you charge too much on your credit card,* [comma] **you will be sorry.**
3) *Because Rosetta Stone speaks three languages,* [comma] **she works well with foreign exchange students.**

Reminder:
Reverse the clauses in the sentences above and the comma disappears.

Example: **You will be sorry** *if you charge too much on your credit card.*

LEVEL ONE EXERCISE 9.3

Mark "yes" if the item is correctly punctuated with the comma. Mark "no" if the item is incorrectly punctuated.

_____1) Even though I studied like a microscope, I failed the quiz.

_____2) My son cried on the first day of school even though I stayed with him.

_____3) Because I was confused, I did the wrong assignment.

_____4) I missed my first class because my car broke down.

_____5) When I graduate from college, I am going to Hawaii.

LEVEL TWO EXERCISE 9.3

Correct the punctuation in each item below, if necessary.

1) Because the king cobra can grow to over twelve feet it is the largest of the world's poisonous snakes.

2) Meat and potatoes will keep you alive unless you need variation in your diet.

3) Whenever Joe Clown picks up a music box he is certain to overwind it.

4) If you take a walk through a cow pasture you must stay alert for meadow muffins.

5) Professor Wordy started talking, as soon as he got to the door of the classroom.

9.4 Subordination

Subordination, like **coordination**, is another technique for showing the reader how clauses are related.

Subordination makes a clause — a complete idea — subordinate or less important than some other idea.

Example:
...Fred became interested in physical therapy...

This is an independent clause, a main idea, and to it we can add a lessor idea, a subordinated idea, which is a related thought, but not as important as the main one.

Example:

...Fred became interested in physical therapy...*after he read about that career field...*

(The main or stressed idea is in the independent clause; the subordinate, or less important, idea is in the dependent clause.)

SUBORDINATING CONJUNCTIONS:

The subordinating conjunctions listed below are among the most common.

after	since	whenever	although
as soon as	when	because	even though
before	while	if	unless

Place any one of them in front of a complete thought and you have subordinated that thought:

Example:
...after the meeting was over...

The subordinator *"after"* indicates that a more important point is going to be made, like this:

Example:

...after the meeting was over, **the CEO had a heart attack...**

(Clearly, the "heart attack" clause is the more important idea.)

UNSUBORDINATED WRITING:

> My flaky Aunt Lily Upp believes that people are basically thieves. She will allow no one into her rose garden. She believes that flowers are not to be picked. Everybody she knows cuts flowers. The rose garden comes into bloom. Auntie Upp stands guard. I visit her during the summer, and I may look at her roses from over the gate. I may not touch or smell them.

The writing does not flow smoothly because the writer isn't showing the reader how the ideas are related to each other. Which of these clauses are meant to be stressed, and which are less important? Subordination, where appropriate, can help the reader follow a train of thought more easily.

SUBORDINATED WRITING:

> Because my flaky Aunt Lily Upp believes that people are basically thieves, she will allow no one into her rose garden. She also believes that flowers are not to be picked although everybody she knows cuts flowers. As soon as the rose garden comes into bloom, Auntie Upp stands guard. Whenever I visit her during the summer, I may look at her roses from over the gate, but I may not touch or smell them.

The more important ideas, the ones the writer wishes to stress, are in the independent clauses. The subordinated clauses lead up to those ideas the writer is stressing, or they add a related but less important thought to a main idea.

Complex or Subordinated Sentence Formulas

It may be easier to remember the formulas for the subordinated or complex sentence:

1)   Subject + Verb — Subordinating Conjunction Subject + Verb.
Independent Clause (because, if, while, etc)   Dependent Clause
S+ V sc S+ V.

2)   Subordinating Conjunction Subject + Verb, — Subject + Verb.
(Because, If, While, etc.) Dependent Clause,   Independent Clause
Sc S+ V, S + V.

3)   Subject — Subordinating Conjunction Subject + Verb — Verb.
First part of Independent Clause (who, which, that) Dependent Clause   End of Independent Clause
S sc S+ V V.

LEVEL ONE EXERCISE 9.4

Insert one of the following subordinating conjunctions into the space provided: *after, as soon as, before, since, when, while, whenever, because, if, although, even though, unless.*

1) _____ you come to class, complete your exercises.

2) I ate a double cheeseburger _____ I am on a diet.

3) _____ a small business owner is not careful, he could lose everything.

4) Sam prepared the chicken wings _____ the entire family asked him to.

5) _____ you see a UFO, call 1-800-UFO-ABOV.

6) _____ he earns a good salary, he cannot afford a BMW.

7) The stock market is not for everyone _____ it is very risky.

8) _____ Professor Idle comes in, everyone shout, BOO!

9) Hairball has been arrogant _____ he was a kitten.

10) _____ the Mississippi floods, thousands of farmers suffer.

LEVEL TWO EXERCISE 9.4

Insert one of the following subordinating conjunctions into the space provided: *after, as soon as, before, since, when, while, whenever, because, if, although, even though, unless.*

1) _____ I considered your application carefully, I decided that you were the right person for this company.

2) Professor Mulish knew that he misspoke _____ all the hands in the class went up.

3) _____ this century began, no one would dream of sparing a forest to save an owl species.

4) _____ the landscaper was searching for moles, squirrels devoured his lunch.

5) Serial killers continue to show up in society _____ they almost always get caught.

6) _____ you exercise regularly, you are going to weigh more than you think.

7) _____ you can get Professor Wordy to pause for a moment, I would like to ask him an important question.

8) _____ the symphony orchestra is supposed to be the city's cultural jewel, nobody wants to give it enough money to survive.

9) Joe Clown watches soap operas that he records on his VCR _____ he gets home from work.

10) _____ the major networks have received vigorous complaints, there will now be warnings before a television show concerning its violence.

Chapter Nine Review Exercises

LEVELS ONE AND TWO 9.1 (clauses)

Identify each item as "I" if it is an independent clause. Identify each item as "D" if it is a dependent clause.

_____ 1) Charles Dickens wrote cleverly plotted novels.

_____ 2) Although the rules of the monastery were broken.

_____ 3) The Grand Canal of Venice is polluted.

_____ 4) Because Professor Daft was frowzy.

_____ 5) Whenever Luciano has to speak English.

_____ 6) I am convinced she is a fuddy-duddy.

_____ 7) When a bull camel begins to froth at the mouth.

_____ 8) The fox terrier is one of the nicest dogs to own.

_____ 9) Professor Mulish has a defective courtesy nerve.

_____ 10) As soon as I found her birdcage.

LEVEL ONE 9.2 (dependent clauses and subordinators)

In the space provided write in a subordinating conjunction that shows the relationship between the clauses [*because, if, even though, after, since, whenever,* etc.]. Follow the example.

1) <u>Because</u> he does not speak English well, you must speak slowly.

2) I look for mail _____ I am near the mailbox.

3) _____ I want to smoke myself to death, I will.

4) Jones will meet us at the door _____ he parks the bus.

5) _____ Professor Daft is rattlebrained, I like him a lot.

LEVEL TWO EXERCISE 9.2 (dependent clauses and subordinators)

In the space provided write in a subordinating conjunction that shows the relationship between the clauses (*because, if, even though, after, since, whenever*, etc.)

1) _____ Charles Darwin, the English naturalist, is very famous, few college students have read his most famous book.

2) _____ you intend to dawdle away the afternoon in the library, you might as well stay in the dorm and visit.

3) The damages to his auto were horrendous _____ a derailed locomotive jumped a ditch and landed on it.

4) Luciano has not talked to his favorite goat _____ he left his father's farm in Sicily two years ago.

5) _____ I arrived at college, I became interested in archeology.

LEVELS ONE AND TWO 9.3 (dependent clause and comma)

Are the following sentences correctly punctuated, yes or no?

_____ 1) Unless you enjoy breathing second-hand smoke, you will have to stay away from the local bars.

_____ 2) Grandfather Casanova says, "Make sure of your friends before you curse your enemies."

_____ 3) If you use too much cayenne pepper in that chili, you will lose control of your vocal cords.

_____ 4) Quite a few believe that Lucrezia Borgia, the famous Renaissance duchess, poisoned people left and right even though there is no evidence.

_____ 5) As soon as we entered the crypt I knew I was in the wrong place.

LEVELS ONE AND TWO 9.4 (subordinators)

Insert one of the following subordinating conjunctions into the space provided: *after, as soon as, before, since, when, while, whenever, because, if, although, even though, unless.*

1) _____ Professor Cloudy goes to movies quite often, he never remembers them.

2) I enjoyed watching the strange people pass by _____ I was standing in the middle of the exotic bazaar.

3) _____ the beach is very clean, I will not swim there.

4) Professor Daft said that the horizon was just beyond the horizon_____ he wanted to confuse us.

5) _____ he was still awake at 2 a.m., Senator Stalwart got up and read the Constitution.

LEVELS ONE AND TWO EXERCISE: SENTENCE COMBINING

On a separate sheet of paper, combine each of the following sets of sentences twice: combine each set to make a compound (coordinate sentence) and combine each set to make a complex (subordinate) sentence. Follow the example:

Harry likes pizza.
He eats it every day.
COMPOUND: Harry likes pizza, *so* he eats it every day.
COMPLEX: *Because* Harry likes pizza, he eats it every day.

1. Jack had trouble with the radiator in his car.
    He drove the car to the local garage.

2. Mary was outside raking leaves.
    Her mother was in the kitchen making chicken soup.

3. My mother and I enjoy going to the movies.
    We go every Friday night after dinner.

4. Niagara Falls is a major tourist attraction in both New York State and Canada.
    It is often taken for granted by the residents.

5. Sisyphus pushed the stone up one side of the hill.
    The stone rolled down the other side.

6. Mary threw the eye of newt into the boiling pot.
    The pot bubbled and burped.

7. Knowing your limitations is one sign of maturity.
    Exceeding those limitations is another sign of maturity.

8. The best things in life are free.
    There is a tax on leaving them to your heirs.

9. The twist was a popular dance in the fifties.
    It was easy to do.

10. People with positive attitudes tend to live longer.
    Grouches make themselves sick at a young age.

Chapter Ten

Run-ons and Comma Splices

FIVE WAYS TO CORRECT RUN-ONS AND COMMA SPLICES:

10.1 create two sentences

10.2 comma + short connector

10.3 use a semi-colon

10.4 semi-colon + long connector + comma

10.5 subordinate

A run-on is two sentences which are written together with no punctuation or connecting word between them:

Example: Fred met his professor at nine o'clock they went over the chapter together.

Notice that the above run-on contains two INDEPENDENT CLAUSES. Both of them can stand alone as independent sentences.

A comma splice is similar to a run-on, except that a comma is used to connect the two independent ideas.

Example: Fred reviewed the difficult chapter with his professor, he felt better about the upcoming exam.

REMINDER: Remember that an independent clause is a group of words which contains a subject and a verb, and which expresses a complete idea. Therefore, an independent clause is a sentence.

Example: Fred met his professor at nine o'clock.

Why does a good writer avoid run-ons and comma splices? Read the following:

Mrs. Counterpane

The waiter saw that Mrs. Counterpane was furiously eating her hat was on the floor next to her asparagus salad filled the large dish in front of her assaulting her meal is a better word than eating the waiter turned aside his face in disgust between his teeth he hissed to himself that Mrs. Counterpane was a first class pig hell could not be worse than this dried mashed potato clung to her eyebrow. The waiter never hated his job more than when he served gluttons like this lady fork and knife were flashing like sparks at her table as she ate customers began to notice her animal-like behavior over her food, more than one patron walked out with her fingers Mrs. Counterpane lifted the custard pie to her mouth, standing at the kitchen door the waiter threw up his hands in frustration and anger at her table this horrid old woman sat back finally and burped loudly over the tired waiter's face was written, "Murder the witch!"

An exaggeration? Yes, but the point should be clear. If a writer is careless and produces run-ons and comma splices he creates confusion for the reader.

10.1 USE A PERIOD AFTER THE FIRST CLAUSE AND CREATE TWO SENTENCES

NOT: Professor Blur has weak eyes he squints.
RATHER: Professor Blur has weak eyes. He squints.

NOT: Sasha comes from Siberia, she is happy to be here.
RATHER: Sasha comes from Siberia. She is happy to be here.

LEVEL ONE EXERCISE 9.1

Write RO for run-on, CS for comma splice or C for correct sentence.

_____ 1. Mr. Impulse shops often, he buys what he does not need.

_____ 2. I found a horseshoe it was right on the sidewalk.

_____ 3. The grass was overgrown the bushes were not trimmed.

_____ 4. Nobody in the neighborhood liked Mr. Phew he had no friends.

_____ 5. Word processors can be confusing.

_____ 6. Rosetta Stone resembles her mother, they even dress alike.

_____ 7. At twelve noon the sun is overhead.

_____ 8. Let's go to the races and spend the day.

_____ 9. The saber-toothed tiger is now extinct, it had dental problems.

_____ 10. Soul food is delicious I can't get enough of it.

LEVEL TWO EXERCISE 10.1

Write RO for run-on, CS for comma splice, or C for correct sentence.

_____ 1. Calling someone sophomoric is an insult it means a person is intellectually pretentious or immature.

_____ 2. Music is a part of almost everyone's life, the person who does not like music is rare indeed.

_____ 3. Job hunting is an activity that can be depressing, the seeker must be persistent.

_____ 4. The Fourth of July is America's great holiday it is a time of good food, fine friends, and great fireworks.

_____ 5. The evidence in a well-written mystery novel must not be too obscure, or the reader will feel cheated.

_____ 6. Professor Cloudy scheduled his exam for the day before recess his students were annoyed.

_____ 7. Chicken fricassee is a sure cure for homesickness.

_____ 8. It is impossible to argue with a defective parking meter the driver is never right, the meter always is.

_____ 9. Parenthetic remarks are possible in a research paper they should, however, be kept to a minimum.

_____ 10. The Taj Mahal, built at Agra, India, is considered by many to be the most beautiful building in the world.

10.2 JOIN TWO INDEPENDENT CLAUSES WITH A COMMA + A SHORT CONNECTOR (AND, BUT, SO, OR, NOR, FOR, YET)

(Review the Chapter Eight on coordination and coordinating conjunctions.)

NOT: I read a novel by Stephen King, I liked it very much.
RATHER: I read a novel by Stephen King, and I liked it very much.

NOT: Buy your books early you will be ready for class.
RATHER: Buy your books early, so you will be ready for class.

NOT: The carpenter came to the house he did not stay for long.
RATHER: The carpenter came to the house, but he did not stay for long.

LEVEL ONE EXERCISE 10.2

Place a comma + a short connector (coordinating conjunction) in each of the sentences below. Follow the example in Number 1.

1) There are many ancient cities in Europe, **and** they are all interesting places to visit.

2) Buy a computer if you can, you will need it for schoolwork.

3) *Time* magazine is a good source of information I can't afford it.

4) Professor Wordy talks a lot he is a good teacher.

5) Smoking is dangerous people still do it.

6) We ate a pound of chicken wings, after that we ordered a large pizza.

7) You can come to the church service, you can come to the reception.

8) The anchovy is a small fish some people love to eat them.

9) He did not get the job he enlisted in the army.

10) You missed the quiz on Thursday, you may take it on Monday.

LEVEL TWO EXERCISE 10.2

Place a comma + a short connector (coordinating conjunction) in each of the sentences below. Follow the example in Number 1.

1) My cat, Hairball, is very destructive, and he seems to enjoy being a pest.

2) Ms. Placid went to see an action-packed movie she was bored throughout.

3) The blizzard made driving impossible, we stayed home all day and watched television.

4) Alexander the Great was considered to be a superb general he was never defeated.

5) The choice is yours: you may take a 2-hour test in class, you may do an open book quiz at home.

6) Alfred Hitchcock always looked very serious he was one of the funniest of people.

7) Roman numerals are still used for limited purposes, some people think they should be dispensed with.

8) Professor Portly got caught in the doorway the students had a good laugh.

9) We wanted to see one of those enormous glaciers in Alaska, we booked passage on a northbound steamer.

10) Dinosaurs are everybody's favorite reptiles Hollywood has always made a great deal of money out of this fact.

10.3 USE A SEMI-COLON TO JOIN TWO INDEPENDENT CLAUSE, ESPECIALLY IF THEY ARE CLOSELY RELATED.

NOT: February weather is not good we often have blizzards.
RATHER: February weather is not good; we often have blizzards.

NOT: Submit your papers by the 26th, they will not be accepted late.
RATHER: Submit your papers by the 26th; they will not be accepted late.

LEVEL ONE EXERCISE 10.3

Write RO for run-on, CS for comma splice or C for correct sentence. Correct any errors with the semi-colon.

_____ 1. The office is closed come back on Wednesday.

_____ 2. Mathematics is difficult for Sam, biology is easy.

_____ 3. The Ganges is unpleasant it is highly polluted.

_____ 4. Coffee prices have gone up; consumption has dropped.

_____ 5. My computer paper is cheap, it tears too easily.

LEVEL TWO EXERCISE 10.3

Write RO for run-on, CS for comma splice, or C for correct sentence. Correct any errors with the semi-colon.

_____ 1. Many students at the college are short of funds, they must be made aware of what the financial aid office can offer.

_____ 2. Swimming in Lake Erie can be quite dangerous squalls can blow up within minutes.

_____ 3. Prejudice remains one of the human race's most persistent characteristics; it is the unusual person who has not been guilty of pre-judging.

_____ 4. The python is a member of the constrictor family of snakes, it can grow to twenty feet or more.

_____ 5. Most of the people in my neighborhood speak Spanish I have enrolled in night school to study the language.

10.4 JOIN TWO RELATED INDEPENDENT CLAUSES WITH A SEMI-COLON + A LONG CONNECTOR + A COMMA.

;however,   ;in addition,   ;therefore,   ;as a result,   ;consequently,
;for example, ;furthermore,   ;besides,   ;nevertheless, ;also,

(There are many more of these long connectors called conjunctive adverbs or transitional connectives. They are more formal than the short connectors in 8.3, and they provide a strong sense of transition. See p. 73.)

NOT: I do not like chemistry I will not major in science.
RATHER: I do not like chemistry; therefore, I will not major in science.

NOT: Professor Bustling seems busy, if you ask him for an appointment you will get it.
RATHER: Professor Bustling seems busy; however, if you ask him for an appointment you will get it.

NOT: The local zoo has raised several million dollars recently, the state government has given a large grant.
RATHER: The local zoo has raised several million dollars recently; in addition, the state government has given a large grant.

LEVEL ONE EXERCISE 10.4

Correct the following run-ons and comma splices with appropriate long connectors. Remember the specific punctuation that goes along with them. (E.g. *;therefore, ;nevertheless,*) Follow the example.

1) I did not study well for that exam**; consequently,** I failed it.

2) The senator was caught stealing he was not re-elected.

3) I should have a physical exam, I don't want to spend the money.

4) The students were told not to mark their texts they did it anyway.

5) The Yorkshire terrier needs daily grooming, it's a joy to own.

6) "Zonked" is a slang term meaning drunk, "plastered" means the same thing.

7) His teeth are full of cavities, he will not see a dentist.

8) Professor Flush bought a new car, he bought a yacht, too.

9) Jones worked hard in college he graduated magna cum laude.

10) It rained all summer, my tomato plants rotted.

LEVEL TWO EXERCISE 10.4

On a separate piece of paper correct the following run-ons and comma splices first with a short connector, then with the appropriate long one.

Example: The President did not fulfill his campaign promises he lost much of his middle class support.

      The President did not fulfill his campaign promises, so he lost much of his middle class support.

      The President did not fulfill his campaign promises; consequently, he lost much of his middle class support.

1) The billboard was supposed to be removed within thirty days, three months went by and it was still there.

2) John Q. Student was absent for fifty percent of his classes his professor asked him to withdraw.

3) The larger nations insisted strongly on a new policy of monetary reform, the smaller nations agreed.

4) The car dealer was forced to close his doors, he was given two weeks to reimburse his unhappy customers.

5) Professor Ample was told to stop eating high calorie foods he continued to do so.

6) The municipal building was destroyed by the terrorists the town library was badly damaged.

7) Mr. Faulty has not filed his income tax returns for the last three years, he will spend some time in prison.

8) Assisting terminally ill patients to end their own lives is occurring more often, many people are against this practice.

9) American car manufacturers lose sales to foreign imports every year, more emphasis is being placed on American car quality.

10) Ali Akbar says his country, Iran, encourages study abroad, he is in the United States to study medicine.

10.5 LEAVE ONE CLAUSE INDEPENDENT AND SUBORDINATE THE OTHER

Subordination and subordinating conjunctions (see p. 85)

after	since	whenever	although
as soon as	when	because	even though
before	while	if	unless

You may use a subordinating conjunction to repair a run-on or a comma splice. Remember that a subordinator will make one of the clauses dependent.

REMINDER: Use a comma to separate clauses when the Dependent Clause comes first.

NOT: He graduated from college he joined the Marines.
RATHER: After he graduated from college, he joined the Marines.

NOT: Joe Clown came to the rehearsal he got off from work.
RATHER: Joe Clown came to the rehearsal as soon as he got off from work.

NOT: Luciano was born in Italy, he has a heavy accent.
RATHER: Because Luciano was born in Italy, he has a heavy accent.

NOT: He wrote an insulting letter to the editor he was annoyed with a newspaper article.
RATHER: He wrote an insulting letter to the editor whenever he was annoyed with a newspaper article.

LEVEL ONE EXERCISE 10.5

Correct the following run-ons and comma splices with appropriate subordinating conjunctions. Use the comma when a dependent clause comes first in the sentence. Follow the example.

1) **Unless** you study regularly, you won't remember the material.

2) Fred was warned to stay away, he showed up anyway.

3) The meeting was over, the barbecue began.

4) The college was closed, we had a severe snowstorm.

5) I spilled all of the popcorn I was watching television.

6) I write letters to you will you write back?

7) Professor Idle fell asleep, the exam was over.

8) He was washing his cat his dog got out the front door.

9) John Q. Student received an award his QPA was 4.0.

10) I go to the movies, the audience irritates me.

LEVEL TWO EXERCISE 10.5

Correct the following run-ons and comma splices with appropriate subordinating conjunctions. Use a comma when the dependent clause comes first in the sentence. Follow the example.

1) **Because** the President is under constant attack from the opposing party, he is very careful with the wording of his proposals.

2) Thunder and lightning surprise you on a golf course do not take shelter under a tree.

3) The ballplayers wanted much more money, they were millionaires.

4) The office workers were busy arguing thieves made off with their computers.

5) There is improvement in your grades, you will not be accepted by the college of your choice.

6) My cat, Hairball, is aloof and independent-minded I still can't imagine life without him.

7) Professor Daft canceled the upcoming exams he discovered his answer key was missing.

8) Mr. Quarrles presented his arguments in as vigorous a manner as possible, he lost the debate and was thrown out of the Quibblers' Society.

9) Senator Stalwart is viciously aggressive he feels that is the best way to get things done.

10) Acid rain was not a problem in the United States, the conservationists became alarmed at the dying forests and expiring lakes.

LEVEL TWO CHAPTER REVIEW EXERCISE:

Correct the following run-ons and comma splices with any one of the five methods given:

10.1 create two sentences
10.2 comma + short connector
10.3 use a semi-colon
10.4 semi-colon + long connector + comma
10.5 subordinate

1) The present royal family of England goes back a thousand years many Britishers are proud of that tradition.

2) Salmon can live in the ocean for many years, they must swim up fresh water rivers and streams to spawn.

3) "Schlock" is a very useful slang term, it means something cheap or grossly inferior.

4) He was strongly interested in learning to fly he could not due to his health.

5) The college was closed for the spring recess it burned to the ground.

6) A bungee jumper must have complete faith in the elastic cord around her ankles, it helps to be fearless.

7) Alaska is a spectacular place to visit as the saying goes I wouldn't want to live there.

8) The students have been asked many times graffiti is still appearing on the outside of campus buildings.

9) The breath of a full grown walrus can unsettle maggots this animal should not be kept in the home.

10) The local natives spent hours making baskets in the evening, they had hundreds to sell when the tourists arrived.

11) Betty Crackers enjoys baking cookies her house is full of them at all times.

12) Burning trash to generate electricity is objected to by many the burning often causes extreme pollution.

13) Professor Mulish had a reputation for being stubborn once he made a decision nothing could make him change his mind.

14) Lightning can strike twice in the same place, few people believe it.

15) Loggers have one of the most difficult jobs they must endure the forceful criticisms of conservationists.

16) The Siberian tiger is the largest cat in the world a mature male is taller and weighs much more than a fully-grown lion.

17) Mr. Harper listens to Mozart he will tolerate no interruptions.

18) NASA scientists are planning to send mobile rockets to Mars to collect rocks the government is not enthusiastic.

19) Having a personal computer in the home is said to result in better grades for children, many families cannot afford one.

20) The President introduced his Children's Immunization Proposal there were objections as expected.

LEVEL ONE REVIEW EXERCISE

Rewrite the following paragraph on a separate sheet of paper, and correct the run-ons and comma splices.

(1)The most dangerous person in the world is a klutz. (2)Everyone knows a klutz, a klutz trips over a blade of grass. (3)A klutz is dangerous in a restaurant the klutz spills the water, trips the waitress, and flings food everywhere. (4)A klutz is even dangerous in his or her own house. a tool of any kind becomes a dangerous weapon in the hands of a klutz. (5)Something as harmless as a spoon or a thread can become a lethal weapon in the hands of a klutz. (6)The klutz can snap the spoon right into the picture window and break it. the klutz pulls the thread until the entire garment unravels. (7)The most dangerous place for a klutz is behind the wheel of a car. (8)The klutz will try to dodge a bee inside his or her car; the car swerves off the road and into a ditch. (9)There is no safe place for a klutz. (10)Anyone can be a klutz it is best to be prepared.

LEVEL TWO REVIEW EXERCISE

Rewrite the following paragraph on a separate sheet of paper, and correct the run-ons and comma splices.

(1)There are several advantages to using a word processing program on a computer. (2)One advantage is the ability to use different typefaces or fonts. The writer can also use italics or bold or other types of variations to make the writing more interesting. (3)Another advantage is being able to move text one sentence or paragraph can be moved anywhere on the page. (4)This can save the writer valuable time, he or she does not have to copy the whole thing over. (5)A third advantage is the use of graphics a picture can be inserted anywhere to make the text clearer. (6)Pictures, however, should be used sparingly, too many graphics can obscure the writing. (7)A fourth advantage is the use of a spell checker. (8)Even the best speller can make mistakes the computer program will search through the writing and suggest corrections. (9)However, no spell checker can help the writer with homonyms, Homonyms are words that sound the same but have different meanings. (10)One of the major advantages of a computer is the ability to save the writing onto a disk. (11)The writer never has to worry about the dog chewing up the document there is always another copy on the computer.

Chapter Eleven

Fragments

Definition: **A sentence fragment is an UNFINISHED thought or idea punctuated as a sentence.**

Examples:
1) Jumped over the puddle.
2) Fred along with his sister.
3) Behind the car with the flat tire.
4) Being unhappy in his marriage.
5) After the mechanic broke his arm.
6) Such as tomatoes, celery, and carrots.

Occasionally, excellent writers will use a sentence fragment deliberately, usually for emphasis. However, student writers should avoid fragments, for they can cause CONFUSION.

Example: As soon as possible you must see Professor Cloudy. Who is your instructor.

Is a question being asked here? Or should the last four words be joined to the others? A reader can determine what the fragment means, but fragments slow him down, and that is irritating.

TYPES OF FRAGMENTS:

11.1 missing subject fragment

11.2 missing verb fragment

11.3 "ing" fragment

11.4 phrase fragment

11.5 dependent clause fragment

11.6 "such as" fragment

11.1 The Missing Subject Fragment

Definition: The subject is not there. Remember, every sentence you write must have a subject present. (Command sentences are the only exceptions.)

Examples: Was making an omelet in the kitchen. (Who was making the omelet?)
Saw him running like an ostrich with the police in hot pursuit. (Who saw him running?)

LEVELS ONE AND TWO EXERCISE 11.1

Provide the missing subject in each of the following.

1) Served loyally in World War II.

2) Printed out the documents in the cellar.

3) Succeeded in making Mr. Gallstone bitter.

4) Was praised excessively.

5) Will be given the second prize.

11.2 The Missing Verb Fragment

Definition: The verb is not there. There might be a missing main verb or a missing helping verb.

Examples: Grandfather Casanova in World War II. (What about Grandfather Casanova?)
Bovine Committee voting on the issue. (What about the Bovine Committee?)
The college must its tuition for the fall. (What must the college do?)

LEVELS ONE AND TWO EXERCISE 11.2

Provide the missing verb in each of the following.

1) The mosquitoes so vicious we had to run.

2) I into the cathedral and took many pictures.

3) My motor home speed when climbing a hill.

4) You a lot of nerve!

5) Mr. Debased and Professor Baffle during the meeting.

11.3 The "-ing" Fragment

Definition: The "ing" fragment often begins with a verb ending in "ing." Or the fragment contains a verb ending in "ing" with no helping verb. Use caution when starting a sentence with a word ending in "ing." Verbs ending in "ing" need helping verbs. And a subject must be present.

Examples: Sam cooking a sit-down dinner for twelve. (Needs helping verb like *is* or *was*)
Running down the hall and laughing hysterically. (Needs helping verb and subject)
Being responsible for thirteen children. (Needs helping verb and subject)

LEVEL ONE EXERCISE 11.3

Provide the missing helping verb, and/or provide the missing subject.

1) Jones reading when he fell asleep.

2) Seeing his accuser for the first time.

3) Agreeing with what Raj said.

4) Doing his essay at the last minute.

5) Professor Idle caught napping in the lounge.

LEVEL TWO EXERCISE 11.3

Provide the missing helping verb, and/or provide the missing subject.

1) Waiting nervously for the dentist to see her.

2) Being quick to criticize, Mr. Wasp always stinging somebody.

3) I got very sleepy while I researching my report.

4) Looking to the left as he approached the cliff's edge.

5) Being very talkative about his upcoming divorce.

11.4 The Phrase Fragment

Definition: A phrase punctuated as a sentence is not a complete thought.

Examples: Over the river and through the trees.
From the President of the United States.
Behind in his work.

Remember: A phrase is a group of words without a subject or a verb. (See Chapter Seven)
Every sentence you write must contain a subject and a verb. Phrases, such as prepositional phrases,
are parts of sentences.

LEVELS ONE AND TWO EXERCISE 11.4

Make each of the following a complete sentence by providing the missing subjects and verbs.

1) Between New York and Philadelphia.

2) Into the distant mountains.

3) Through the sound barrier.

4) Around the edges of his country estate.

5) Within the covers of that book.

6) Upon further investigation.

7) Down the corridor, through the double doors, and out the window.

8) Before his speech and because of the mood of the crowd.

9) From the darkest corners of the dismal attic.

10) Just to his left and over his head.

11.5 The Dependent Clause Fragment

Definition: A dependent clause punctuated like a sentence does not contain a complete thought.

Examples: As long as you are going to Nevada.
Before you register for biology.
Since Joe Clown has all the answers.

REMINDER: A subordinate, dependent clause cannot stand by itself as a sentence. IT MUST BE ATTACHED TO AN INDEPENDENT CLAUSE. (See Chapter 9.) Remember the words that subordinate: after, as soon as, before, since, when, while, whenever, because, if, although, even though, unless.
Note: The relative pronouns (who, which, that) can also function as subordinating conjunctions.

LEVEL ONE EXERCISE 11.5

Study each set of sentences below. If you discover a dependent clause fragment, identify and correct it. **REMINDER:** When a dependent clause comes first, it is followed by a comma (just like this sentence).

1a) John Q. Student was not ready for his exam. 1b)Although he had to take it. 1c)John was very worried.

2a) If you go to Room 16, you will find it locked. 2b)Nobody has looked inside for years. 2c)Even though strange noises have been heard from behind the door.

3a) Professor Ample eats too much. 3b)Because he has very little self-control.

4a) A supernova is an exploding star. 4b)Which glows brightly in the evening sky.

5a) While we were waiting for Professor Cash. 5b)Lightning burned a hole through the classroom ceiling. 5c)Professor Cash was not amused.

LEVEL TWO EXERCISE 11.5

Study each set of sentences below. If you discover a dependent clause fragment, identify and correct it. **REMINDER:** When a dependent clause comes first, it is followed by a comma (just like this sentence).

1a) Rosetta Stone is a linguist. 1b)Although she is not particularly intelligent.

2a) As long as you have patience and can listen quietly. 2b)Grandfather Casanova will be your devoted friend. 2c)Interrupt him and you're in danger.

3a) While the conservatives were trying to overthrow the government. 3b)The liberals were looting the treasury. 3c)And the middle-of-the-roaders were on holiday.

4a) When the king cobra strikes, its venom immediately attacks the nervous system, and death can come within minutes, even for a human. 4b)This snake is a particular problem in India.

5a) Because Hairball, my cat, does not care very much for people. 5b)I must throw him into the cellar. 5c)When company comes to visit.

6a) Professor Blur cannot get along with his computer. 6b)If I show him how to create a file and save it. 6c)He frets that he will forget the instructions. 6d)Which he does.

7a) Ali Akbar has nerve fibers made out of steel cables. 7b)Since he loves bungee jumping. 7c)He jumps as often as he can. 7d)Whenever he has enough money.

8a) If you want to meet an interesting person. 8b)Strike up a conversation with Senator Stalwart. 8c)He will impress you with what he knows about politicians. 8d)Who mess up the government.

9a) Before Mr. Faulty was permitted to purchase the old church building, he had to promise in writing to make repairs. 9b)He had a problem understanding this. 9c)Because he planned to tear the structure down.

10a) Unless the Lardo Society moves into new facilities. 10b)Some of the membership have threatened to break away and start their own club. 10c)The floor in the society's present building is threatening to collapse.

11.6 The "Such As" Fragment

Definition: The type of fragment begins with "such as" or "for example" followed by a series.

Examples: Some purebred dogs are ugly. Such as the bulldog, the boxer, and the mastiff.
Many science courses are available. For instance chemistry, physics, and biology.
I am interested in seeing two cities in Italy. Specifically Florence and Rome.

Solution: Join the above fragments to the previous sentence with a comma.
Some purebred dogs are ugly, such as the bulldog, the boxer, and the mastiff.

LEVELS ONE AND TWO EXERCISE 10.6

Correct the "such as" fragments in the following.

1) Mr. Impulse buys amazing junk. For instance a "magic" lantern, a used Roman candle, and one left shoe.

2) Two people were fired this morning. Namely Mr. Livermore and Mr. Debased.

3) Jones is very good with Romance languages. Such as Spanish, French, and Italian.

4) Joe Clown made some personal resolutions. For example to get more sleep, to earn more money, and to study less often.

5) The police placed several charges against Mr. Gallstone. Specifically assault and battery, leaving the scene of an accident, and resisting arrest.

For Your Information

Some professional writers will occasionally use a fragment to emphasize an idea.

Chapter 11 Review Exercises

LEVELS ONE AND TWO REVIEW EXERCISE:

Study each set of sentences below. If you discover no fragment, mark C for correct in the space provided. If you discover a sentence fragment, mark SF in the space provided and make the necessary correction.

_____ 1. Feeling the way you do is wrong. I believe you should see Professor Bustling and discuss the issue. What do you think?

_____ 2. Many dolphins are being caught in nets which fishermen put out for tuna. The dolphins die and are dumped back into the ocean. Are against this practice and they are fighting it.

_____ 3. I am gaining too much weight. Which is why I have stopped putting butter on my popcorn. I use margarine instead.

_____ 4. Even though I told Mr. Impulse the styrofoam vase was badly done and worthless. He refused to listen. And spent twenty dollars on another piece of rubbish.

_____ 5. Pompeii was a fascinating ruin to visit. Although it was raining that day and most of the tourists were complaining. Going back as soon as possible.

_____ 6. Professor Baffle says he has too many ailments. For example a sore back, sensitive teeth, weak knees, falling hair, and warts.

_____ 7. The secretary got lost in the company warehouse. Among the acres of stored filing cabinets on the second floor. Now she has nightmares.

_____ 8. Betty Crackers is sure she is a better cook than Sam. Although Sam has won many international cooking awards. He is also a graduate of the Cordon Bleu cooking school in Paris. Which annoys Betty a lot.

_____ 9. Down the alley, out into the street, and across the square. The boys were running as fast as possible after the mugger. Who snatched Auntie Upp's purse.

_____ 10. The tuba player has special problems with his instrument during a parade. Especially on a windy day.

⟨LEVELS ONE AND TWO REVIEW EXERCISE:

On a separate sheet of paper, rewrite the following paragraph and correct the fragments.

(1) Curiosity is an attribute of the successful student. (2) Too many students do not approach subject matter with a healthy interest. (3) In finding out more about the subject. (4) This lack of curiosity. (5) Leads to boredom, inattention, and poor work habits. (6) If a student brings some healthy curiosity to a subject. (7) He or she is more likely to do better on homework assignments, find the subject matter involving and learn more about the subject. (8) For example, a liberal arts major who takes a computer course. (9) Will do well in the course. (10) If he or she is curious about computers and how they work. (11) This doesn't mean the liberal arts major will become a computer expert. (12) Although that is possible. (13) It does mean that the liberal arts major will enjoy the course. (14) And get more out of it. (15) One technique for re-kindling this kind of curiosity. (16) Is to find something in every course that is appealing. (17) It might be the movement of tectonic plates in an earth science course. (18) Or a Shakespearean sonnet that speaks to the student's heart. (19) No matter what the interest. (20) The student should read more than just the assigned text. (21) The student should go to the library. (22) And look up more material on the subject. (23) The student can also ask the instructor for further reading material. (24) It is this kind of curiosity. (25)That makes learning a lifelong joy.

LEVEL TWO REVIEW EXERCISE:

Locate the various types of sentence fragments and correct them on a separate sheet of paper.

(1) Grandfather Casanova had never been on a whale-watching expedition before, and he was looking forward to it. (2) On the day of the trip. (3) He excitedly approached the wharf where the ship was docked. (4) Feeling his heart beat was faster than normal. (5) He had been on ships before today, of course. (6) Such as battle ships, ocean liners, and freighters. (7) However, he did not trust an ocean-going vessel as small as this whale-watching boat. (8) Even though it could carry more than one hundred passengers. (9) After boarding the vessel and finding a place to sit on the top deck. (10) Grandfather Casanova thought about the ship's name, *The Jeopardy*. (11) Which did not help to relax the old fellow. (12) At last the ship was on its way. (13) Speeding out to where whales were known to feed. (14) After a short run of thirty minutes, the captain suddenly cut the engines. (15) Calling out, "Humpback at 10 o'clock!" (16) Immediately, the 100 passengers all lunged for the left-hand side of the vessel. (17) Which leaned dramatically. (18) A tremendous whale loomed up out of the sea off to port. (19) As a chorus of cameras clicked away rapidly. (20) The ship leaned and leaned, but a crewman called out that it was normal, and the ship was built for it. (21) Grandfather Casanova could not get up from his seat. (22) Without falling over. (23) This went on all afternoon, as the crowd dashed from rail to rail like idiots. (24) When whales were spotted. (25) Constantly the ship leaned and listed and tipped like a drunken sailor. (26) Clung to his seat for the entire trip, saw no whales at all, and said, "Never again!"

LEVEL ONE AND LEVEL TWO REVIEW EXERCISE
CHAPTERS TEN AND ELEVEN:

In the spaces provided, identify each of the following as correct (C), comma splice (CS), fragment (SF) or run-on (RO).

(1) Once upon a time in a galaxy far far away. (2) There lived an android named George. (3) George's fondest wish was to become a human, he went to visit a wizard named Id. (4) Id, who was very well known throughout the galaxy. (5) Was busy preparing for an upcoming convention of wizards. (6) George knocked on his door the wizard opened the door. (7) George explained his problem, and the wizard listened very intently; his eyes were fixed on George. (8) Id nodded, he began to make a potion. (9) After George drank the potion, he began to feel very odd. (10) Ten minutes later, George turned into Tom Selleck.

1. _____   6. _____

2. _____   7. _____

3. _____   8. _____

4. _____   9. _____

5. _____   10. _____

Chapter Twelve

Pronouns

Pronouns are some of the handiest words in our language. They help us keep our ideas straight, if we use them properly, and they avoid annoying repetition of key words, not only in our speech, but also in our writing. Would you write **this**?

> I took my puppy to the vet's this morning because my puppy hurt his front paw. When the vet saw my puppy's front paw, the vet said all my puppy needed was a shot for pain, so the vet gave my puppy an injection and my puppy relaxed immediately.

Most students can see right away that pronouns are needed to avoid this awful repetition, again whether one is speaking or writing. Basic information concerning personal pronouns follows. If you are fairly good with pronouns, you may wish to jump directly into sections 12.5 through 12.8 and review some trouble spots. (See also Chapter Seven)

12.1 pronoun

12.2 antecedent

12.3 number

12.4 person

12.5 personal pronouns & agreement

12.6 indefinite pronouns & agreement

12.7 neither/nor and either/or

12.8 pronouns and collective nouns

12.1 Pronoun

Definition: A pronoun is a word that **replaces** or **refers** to a noun or another pronoun.

Examples:

1) See Mr. Teller because he is the registrar.
("he" replaces "Mr. Teller" and avoids repetition)
2) The girls are in their seats by 8 a.m.
("their" refers to "girls")
3) Luciano passes all of his exams.
("his" refers to "Luciano")

Subject Pronouns: I, you, he, she, it, we, they
Object Pronouns: me, you, him, her, it, us, them

(See also Chapter Seven, pages 58 - 59)

LEVEL ONE EXERCISE 12.1

In each sentence, identify the pronouns and the words they **replace** or **refer** to.

1) Mr. Debased does not want to pay his rent.

2) Her friends did not show up, so Auntie Upp spent the evening pulling weeds.

3) Jones wanted to see *Psycho*, so he rented it.

4) Hairball, my cat, hates to have his ears touched.

5) Pound the pizza dough until it is firm and smooth.

12.2 Antecedent

Definition: The **antecedent** is the word a pronoun replaces or refers to. The antecedent often comes before the pronoun in a sentence, but it may occur after the pronoun.

Examples:

1) Sasha was delighted to see her parents.
("Sasha" is antecedent to "her")
2) When he finished, Elmo left the room.
("Elmo" is antecedent to "he")
3) Policemen usually enjoy their work.
("Policemen" is antecedent to "their")

LEVELS ONE AND TWO EXERCISE 12.2

In each sentence, identify the pronouns and their antecedents.

1) Strangely enough, Mr. Wasp raises bees in his backyard.

2) Orlando and its suburbs are covered with orange trees.

3) Students and their cars are difficult to separate.

4) Senator Stalwart and his cronies are after all major polluters and their bank accounts.

5) Mrs. Counterpane does not care for her relatives, and they are not particularly interested in her.

12.3 Number

Definition: **Number** refers to whether a word is *singular* or *plural*.

This concept is important to remember because pronouns and their antecedents must agree in number.

If the antecedent is *singular* in number, its pronoun must be *singular* also.

If the antecedent is *plural* in number, its pronoun must be *plural* also.
(More about agreement in section 12.5)

Examples:

1) The students handed their papers in to Professor Daft.
("their is plural because "students" is plural)
2) His court is always crowded, and Judge Fossil likes it that way. ("His" is singular because "Judge Fossil" is singular)
3) Everyone is asleep in her seat on the plane.
("her" is singular because "everyone" is singular)

LEVELS ONE AND TWO EXERCISE 12.3

Identify the **number** of each of the following words.

1) their	5) its	9) us
2) nobody	6) his	10) they
3) computers	7) he	11) we
4) design	8) you	12) I

12.4 Person: 1st, 2nd, and 3rd

Remember: The word **person** is often used with pronouns.

1st Person pronouns are the ones a speaker uses to refer to himself, or to a group of which he is a part.
Example:

> As president of this class, I want us all to have a great Homecoming Weekend.
> ("I" and "us" are 1st person pronouns: "I" is singular and "us" is plural)

2nd Person pronouns are the ones a speaker uses to address someone else, either in speech or writing.
Example:

> You tell the lawyer that you want your damaged car fixed immediately.
> ("You" and "your" are 2nd person pronouns)

3rd Person pronouns are the ones a speaker or writer uses to address or to refer to people, places or things.
Examples:

> 1) I told him to put his cigar in the sand bucket, where it would extinguish itself.
> ("him" - "his" - "it" - are all 3rd person pronouns)
> 2) The neighbors came with plenty of food, and they brought their children, too.
> ("they" and "their" are 3rd person pronouns)

REMINDER:
All nouns, singular and plural, are 3rd person words.

LEVELS ONE AND TWO EXERCISE 12.4

Identify the number and person of each of the following words in the space provided.

_____1) them   _____6) your

_____2) records   _____7) I

_____3) Professor Languid   _____8) me

_____4) us   _____9) it

_____5) magazine   _____10) their

12.5 Personal Pronouns and Agreement

In 12.3 we mentioned that pronouns must agree in number with their antecedents —
Remember:

> singular pronouns refer to singular antecedents
> plural pronouns refer to plural antecedents

Also remember that pronouns must agree with their antecedents in number and person:

1ST PERSON SINGULAR **I, me, my, mine**	1ST PERSON PLURAL **we, us, our, ours**
2ND PERSON SINGULAR **You, your, yours**	2ND PERSON PLURAL **you, your, yours**
3RD PERSON SINGULAR **he, him, his she, her, hers it, its**	3RD PERSON PLURAL **they, them their, theirs**

Agreement Examples:

1) Team members must turn in their equipment before Friday.
(3rd person plural "their" agrees with 3rd person plural "members" —
all nouns are 3rd person)

2) I must find the room where my math class is supposed to meet.
("I" and "my" agree in person and number — both are 1st person singular.)

LEVELS ONE AND TWO EXERCISE 12.5

Fill in the appropriate personal pronoun for the underlined antecedent in each sentence.

1) Foreign <u>cars</u> are popular because _____ appear to be very dependable.

2) <u>I</u> stopped in to see _____ dentist because _____ tooth hurt.

3) <u>Professor Cash</u> bought _____ Rolls Royce while_____ was in England.

4) College <u>students</u> want _____ professors to take them seriously.

5) Although <u>Joe Clown</u> gets into trouble, _____ is very likeable.

12.6 Indefinite Pronouns and Agreement

The following indefinite pronouns are always **SINGULAR**:
> **anybody, anyone, anything**
> **each, either, every, everybody, everyone**
> **neither, nobody, no one**
> **somebody, someone, something**

The following indefinite pronouns are sometimes **PLURAL**/sometimes **SINGULAR**:
> **all, any**
> **more, most**
> **none, some**

The agreement rule for writing is the same: personal pronouns must agree in person and number with antecedent indefinite pronouns.

Examples:
> 1) Everybody is hanging up **his** coat.
> 2) Anyone can come if **he** wants to.
> 3) All the children want **their** cake.

A WORD ABOUT *"NONE:"*
Most of the time this word is a singular indefinite pronoun, and verbs (see Chapter Thirteen) and other pronouns must be singular to agree with it.
Examples:
> 1) **None** of the lawyers in the court **is** ready to begin **his** or **her** presentation.
> 2) **None** of the companies **is** ready for expansion.
> 3) **None** of the employees **wants** to lose **his** job.

These sentences may sound strange, but each is formally correct.
Occasionally, "none" can be a plural indefinite pronoun, and it takes plural verbs and pronouns.

Examples:
> 1) The detectives searched for fingerprints; however, **none were** found.
> 2) **None were** in the house, but thousands of ants were under the porch.

Important Note:
...concerning pronoun reference and agreement...
There is a **difference** between how pronouns agree with antecedents in **conversational**
> (Colloquial) English and **formal** English:

IN CONVERSATION:
> Most people would say: Anybody can quit smoking if **they** want to.

IN FORMAL WRITING:
> Notice the change: Anybody can quit smoking if **he** wants to.
> ...or   Anybody can quit smoking if **he** or **she** wants to.

Some people object to the use of masculine "he" when a sentence contains an indefinite pronoun like "anybody" or "everybody" because it appears to leave women out. Some also object to the use of the "he or she" substitute because this pattern can be awkward and repetitive. The English language has no pronoun that means "he or she" so one way out of the problem is to **re-word the sentence** and use a **plural** subject:

> **People** can quit smoking if **they** want to.
> **Students** behind in **their** work should see **their** professors.
> **Drivers** should always wear **their** seatbelts.

IN CONVERSATION:

> **Everyone** of the students are going for **their** break.
> **Each** of the workers are ready for **their** paychecks.
> If a **teenager** wants **their** own phone **they** should pay for it.
> **No one** in **their** right mind will vote for more taxes.

IN FORMAL WRITING:

> **Everyone** of the students is going for **his** break.
> **Each** of the workers is ready for **his or her** paycheck.
> If a **teenager** wants **his** own phone, **he** should pay for it.
> **No one** in **his** right mind will vote for more taxes.

CAUTION! THE INTERVENING PHRASE:

> Watch out for the **intervening phrase**.
> It comes between the subject of a sentence and the verb and/or pronoun, and it can cause agreement problems.
> NOT: Everyone **of the students** are interested in their final grades.
> Rather: Everyone of the students **is** interested in his or her final grades.

The **intervening phrase** "of the students" contains a plural noun, and that noun leads many students to write the plural verb "are" and the plural pronoun "their." But remember — the subject of a sentence is **never** in a prepositional phrase. Therefore, the subject in the above sentence is "Everyone" not "students." The verb must be the singular "is" to agree with the singular indefinite subject pronoun "Everyone." And the pronouns "his or her" must agree with singular "Everyone" as well.

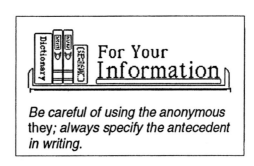

Be careful of using the anonymous they; *always specify the antecedent in writing.*

LEVEL ONE EXERCISE 12.6

Choose the correct pronoun for formal college writing.

1) Everyone is in (their/his) seat.

2) Neither of the students wants to take (their/her) finals.

3) Someone has lost (their/his) concert ticket.

4) No one in the room has enjoyed (their/his or her) dinner.

5) Everybody should have (their/his or her) teeth cleaned.

LEVEL TWO EXERCISE 12.6

Choose the correct pronoun for formal college writing.

1) Anybody who wants (their/his) copy of last year's exam should come up to the front of the room.

2) No one wants to put (their/his) foot in (their/his) mouth and give the wrong answer.

3) Each of the cars in the parking lot had (their/its) tires slashed.

4) Everyone of the athletes was encourage to do (their/his) best for the team.

5) All of the professors had (their/his) personal opinions of the upcoming election.

6) Neither of the employees was interested in (their/his) new co-worker's constant bragging.

7) According to the newspapers, none of the astronomers was accurate in (their/his) predictions of the comet's path.

8) Nobody in the conference room intended to express (their/his) true opinion of the boss's latest policy on lunch hours.

9) Someone in the office had the nerve to help (themselves/himself) to all of the cookies.

10) Judge Fossil said that anyone who wishes to be excused may take (their/his) papers and go.

12.7 "Neither/nor" and "Either/or"

These constructions separate two subjects, and the pronoun **near the second subject** agrees with the second subject in person and number.

Examples:

1) Neither the instruction book nor the maps are in their proper places.
(The pronoun "their" agrees with the second subject "maps")

2) Neither the maps nor the book is in its proper place.
(The pronoun "its" agrees with the second subject "book")

3) Either Professor Blur or the students will drive their cars to Toronto.
(The pronoun "their" agrees with the second subject "students")

4) Either the students or Professor Blur will drive his car to Toronto.
(The pronoun "his" agrees with the second subject Professor Blur.)

LEVELS ONE AND TWO EXERCISE 12.7

Fill in the correct pronoun in the space provided.

1) Either Betty Crackers or Sam will give _____ presentation this evening.

2) Neither the printer nor the computers are in _____ shipping cartons.

3) Either the employees or the owner will open _____ office at 8 a.m.

4) Neither Mr. Faulty nor the Lardo Society will pursue _____ complaints any further.

5) Neither Joe Clown nor his relatives pay _____ bills on time.

12.8 Pronouns and Collective Nouns

Collective nouns in English are usually singular, and singular pronouns refer to them.

Some collective nouns include **team, class, faculty, gang, audience, band, company, collection, crowd, assortment.**

NOT: The class was proud of **their** contribution.
RATHER: The class was proud of **its** contribution.

NOT: The gang is usually found in **their** own territory.
RATHER: The gang is usually found in **its** own territory.

LEVELS ONE AND TWO EXERCISE 12.8

Fill in the correct pronoun in the space provided.

1) The faculty wanted _____ paychecks reissued.

2) The gang was pleased with _____ evil reputation.

3) The audience rocked the building with _____ uproar.

4) The team was surprised at _____ easy victory.

5) The current band was paid more than _____ predecessor.

CHAPTER TWELVE REVIEW EXERCISES

LEVELS ONE AND TWO 12.1 (Pronouns)

In each sentence, identify the pronouns and the words they replace or refer to.

1) Mr. Livermore and Auntie Upp did not like each other, and neither he nor she would say "hello."

2) The chrysanthemum lost its petals; they withered and turned brown.

3) Professor Ample brought us a tray of doughnuts, and we dug in the moment he put it down.

4) Sasha and her sisters, she says, would never tell anyone their ages.

5) The older friars in the monastery spend most of their time in prayer, and they are content to do so.

LEVELS ONE AND TWO 12.2 (Antecedents)

In each sentence, identify the pronouns and their antecedents.

1) Mr. Faulty, when he isn't concentrating, often stumbles over his own two feet.

2) The weeds in Aunt Lily's garden should run for their lives; she goes after them with boiling hot water in her teapot.

3) "Insipid" means dull, uninteresting, or bland. It is a handy word to know.

4) The boys were unhappy with their work; they got too many paper cuts on their hands by stuffing envelopes.

5) Sam made his friends his masterpiece lasagna, and they devoured it.

LEVELS ONE AND TWO EXERCISE 12.3 AND 12.4
(Number and person)

Identify the number (singular or plural) and person (1st, 2nd, 3rd) of the following words. Item 1 is done for you.

<u>plural 1st</u>_____ 1) we   _____ 2) them

_____ 3) ship   _____ 4) me

_____ 5) you   _____ 6) Luciano

_____ 7) her   _____ 8) tools

_____ 9) I   _____10) us

LEVEL ONE EXERCISE 12.5 (Pronoun Agreement)

Fill in the appropriate personal pronoun for the underlined antecedent in each sentence.

1) <u>Mr. Gallstone</u> insulted _____ doctor by calling him a thief.

2) <u>Photographers</u> often complain about the weight of _____ equipment bags.

3) <u>Mr. Wasp</u> said that _____ will not open _____ door

to anyone until _____ landlord fixes the window screens.

4) Elmo's <u>parents</u> said _____ were very proud of _____.

5) My <u>friends and I</u> watched "professional" wrestling on television; _____

were not impressed.

LEVEL ONE EXERCISE 12.6 (Indefinite Pronoun Agreement)

Choose the correct pronoun for formal college writing.

1) None of the students is ready for (their/his or her) exam.

2) Each of the dogs knows (his/its/their) owner.

3) Everyone of the waitresses needs (their/her) tips.

4) Somebody is going to find (their/his) car damaged.

5) Neither of the countries taxes (their/its) people.

LEVEL TWO EXERCISE 12.6 (Indefinite Pronoun Agreement)

Choose the correct pronoun for formal college writing. Also, choose the correct verb (see Chapter Thirteen).

1) Anybody who thinks that (they/he) (are/is) going to be excused from the meeting (are/is) mistaken.

2) Nobody wants people to think that (they/he) (are/is) stupid.

3) Someone in the darkened theater made an impression when (they/he) fired a revolver at the screen.

4) Anyone who is boarding Flight 13 should check (their/his) luggage immediately.

5) Professor Baffle knows somebody who had (their/his) tax return audited.

LEVELS ONE AND TWO EXERCISE 12.7 ("Neither/nor")

Choose the correct pronoun for formal college writing.

1) Neither the bishop nor the priests wanted to give up (their/his) vacation time.

2) Neither the employees nor the manager was interested in helping (their/his) customers.

3) Either the senator or his secretaries demanded that (his/their) office be painted before the weekend.

4) Either the judge or the jurors suggested that (their/his) lunchtime was overdue.

5) Neither the United States nor Russia wants to cut back on (their/its) stockpile of nuclear weapons.

LEVELS ONE AND TWO EXERCISE 12.8
(Collective nouns and Agreement)

Choose the correct pronoun for formal college writing.

1) The constellation of stars was not visible in (their/its) usual place in the eastern sky.

2) We argued about a bundle of used books and (their/its) price.

3) I studied and assortment of South American butterflies in (their/its) cases at the museum.

4) The crew of Professor Cash's yacht was disappointed in (their/its) loss of the Fourth of July race.

5) The soccer team was awarded with a sumptuous dinner for (their/its) victories during (their/its) very first year.

Chapter Thirteen

Subject-Verb Agreement

To avoid confusing the reader, the subject and the verb in a sentence must agree in number. If the subject is singular, the verb that goes with it must be singular. If the subject is plural, the verb must be plural.

13.1 Words between the subject and verb

Be careful not to let words or phrases that come between the subject and verb interfere with agreement. (See page 123 "The Intervening Phrase")
Examples:

The *price* of these new cars **is** too high. (one price = singular)
   subj   verb
The *manager*, along with the players, **is** upset over the loss. (one manager = singular)
   subj   verb

Reminder: Singular verbs in third person end in *"s."*

13.2 Inversions

When the verb comes before the subject, it still agrees with the subject in number.
Examples:

There **is** a good *reason* for his poor attitude.
   verb   subj   ("There" and "here" are never subjects.)
Here **are** the *books* on economics for your class.
   verb   subj

13.3 Singular Subject Pronouns

Some pronouns always take singular verbs. These include **each, either, neither, nobody, one, someone, somebody, no one.** (See page 122 "Indefinite Pronouns")
Examples:

Each of the students **has** five classes for a full load.
subj   verb
Neither of the boys **is** prepared for the final exam.
subj   verb
One of the vacationers **is** lost in space.
subj   verb

13.4 Plural Subject Pronouns

Some pronouns always take plural verbs. These include **both, few, many, several.**
Examples:

Both of the physics exams **were** difficult.
subj   verb
Few of the students **understand** the need for discipline and motivation.
subj   verb

13.5 Two or more subjects joined by the word *"and"*

When two or more subjects are joined by the word *"and,"* the verb is plural.
Examples:

The *snow* and the *wind* **make** driving hazardous in the Northeast.
     subj   subj verb
John and *Mary* **own** several submarine shops.
subj   subj   verb

13.6 Singular nouns ending in *"s"*

Some nouns that end in *"s"* are singular in meaning and take a singular verb.
Examples:

The Buffalo News **is** the only newspaper in Buffalo. (*The Buffalo News* = one newspaper)
    subj   verb
Economics **is** a required course for business majors. (*Economics* = one course)
   subj   verb

13.7 Subjects connected by *"or"/ "nor"*

When there are two or more subjects with an *"or"* or *"nor"* between them, the verb agrees
with the closest subject.
    Examples:

Neither the *students* nor the *teacher* **knows** about the changes in administration.
            subj   subj   verb   (teacher is closer to the verb)
Either the *boss* or the *employees* **are** responsible for the contract dispute.
         subj   subj   verb   (employees is closer to the verb)

13.8 *"A number"* and *"The number"*

When *"a number"* is the subject of the sentence, the verb is plural because the suggestion is
that there is more than one. When *"the number"* is the subject of the sentence, the verb is singular
because the suggestion is that a single number or digit is meant.
    Examples:

A number of students **are** absent.   ("A number" refers to more than one.)
subj   verb
The number of absent students **is** small.   ("The number" refers to one numeral.)
  subj   verb

13.9 Collective nouns

Nouns that refer to groups are called collective nouns and include words such as **class, team, jury, audience.** These nouns may be either singular or plural. The meaning of the sentence is crucial for determining the number implied.

Examples:

The *jury* **is sequestered** for the night. ("Jury" is considered one unit and singular.)
    subj   verb

The *jury* **have been** on their feet all night. ("Jury" refers to the members and is plural.)
    subj   verb

This last example should sound a bit odd to you. One way to avoid this construction and make agreement easier is to use words like **members** that are clearly plural.

The jury *members* **have been** on their feet all night.
    subj   verb

13.10 *"Who," "Which," "That"* as Subject Pronouns

In complex sentences using *who, which* or *that* as subject pronouns, the verb agrees with the subject replaced by *who, which* or *that.*

Examples:

The boy *who* **sits** in the back is my cousin. (*"Who"* refers to boy and boy is singular.)
    subj verb

The medicine *that* **tastes** bitter often works best. (*"That"* refers to medicine and medicine is singular.)
    subj   verb

The books *which* **are** most popular are often least literary. (*"Which"* refers to books and books is plural.)
    subj   verb

For Your Information

The time to check for subject-verb agreement is during your editing process.

LEVEL ONE EXERCISE #1

On the line provided, write the verb that agrees with the subject in each of the following sentences.

_____ 1. A fear of heights (are, is) common.

_____ 2. Behind the bushes (are, is) the trimmer.

_____ 3. Ambition and motivation (are, is) necessary for success.

_____ 4. The captain, as well as the crewmen, (are, is) responsible for the oil spill.

_____ 5. Each of the voters (are, is) exercising the right to democratic choice.

_____ 6. The stack of dishes (are, is) leaning precariously.

_____ 7. Either the boss or the employees (are, is) responsible for production.

_____ 8. There (were, was) many applications for the manager's position.

_____ 9. Dinosaurs (are, is) staging a comeback.

_____ 10. In the drawer with the dirty clothes (are, is) a cheese sandwich.

LEVEL TWO EXERCISE #1

On the line provided, write the verb that agrees with the subject in each of the following.

_____ 1. The way to make money (are, is) to increase production, distribution, and advertising.

_____ 2. The subject of too many Hollywood movies (are, is) violence.

_____ 3. The number of mistakes someone makes (are, is) often used against that person.

_____ 4. Those who (are, is) in the club will pay less than nonmembers to use the golf course.

_____ 5. There (was, were) several minor interruptions during the professor's lecture.

_____ 6. A number of people (believe, believes) that Japan relies too heavily on exports.

_____ 7. The best cure for long evenings (are, is) short naps.

_____ 8. A hamburger with mustard, sauerkraut, and onions (are, is) dangerous.

_____ 9. Juggling chainsaws, machetes and lit torches (are, is) not recommended for the average person.

_____ 10. Far out on the horizon (was, were) the faint outline of the dormant volcano.

_____ 11. Either the maid or the two butlers (was, were) responsible.

_____ 12. Each of the new car models (has, have) the safety features required by law.

_____ 13. The high crime in some neighborhoods (are, is) difficult to stop without cooperation.

_____ 14. Harold, together with Chaplin, (was, were) a silent film comic.

_____ 15. One of the best movies ever made (was, were) *The Wizard of Oz.*

_____ 16. John, Bob, and Bill (want, wants) to date Vanna White.

_____ 17. The pulse of a nation (are, is) found in its people.

_____ 18. He who (laugh, laughs) last at a joke thought about it overnight.

_____ 19. There (is, are) always a list of duties in every job description.

_____ 20. The subjects of Business Law and Statistics (are, is) difficult.

_____ 21. The money that (is, are) wasted on pork barrel projects is shameful.

_____ 22. One of the Seven Wonders of the World (are, is) Niagara Falls.

_____ 23. Everyone who sees Niagara Falls (are, is) struck by its power.

_____ 24. A gridlocked Congress (accomplish, accomplishes) very little.

_____ 25. Having a positive attitude (help, helps) lighten life's load.

Chapter Fourteen

Basic Punctuation

Without basic punctuation, our lives as readers would be confusing, messy, and difficult.

A college education is necessary in todays job market without a degree the person looking for employment is at a distinct disadvantage and often has to take low-paying unskilled jobs high technology requires greater skill for example in the computer field its not enough to know how to turn a computer on its also necessary to know programming language hardware components and software mechanics more advanced technical fields such as robotics require even more education the need for a college education has never been greater than it is today

This paragraph is difficult to follow and confusing at best because it lacks the punctuation necessary to read it. With the punctuation, the paragraph becomes easier to read.

A college education is necessary in today's job market. Without a degree, the person looking for employment is at a distinct disadvantage and often has to take low-paying, unskilled jobs. High technology requires greater skill. For example, in the computer field it's not enough to know how to turn on a computer; it's also necessary to know programming language, hardware components, and software mechanics. More advanced technical fields such as robotics require even more education. The need for a college education has never been greater than it is today.

Three types of internal punctuation (punctuation used inside the sentence) are the **comma**, the **semi-colon** and the **apostrophe**.

14.1 The Comma

The comma's basic purpose is to separate one part of a sentence from another part to make it easier to read. One problem student writers have with the comma is that it can separate many different items, and often it is overused, partly because students have been told to put one wherever they pause. Sometimes, however, students pause in strange places. It's better to learn the conventions of the comma. **There are six basic items a comma can separate:**

(1) two sentences joined by a coordinating conjunction
(2) introductory material from the independent clause
(3) three or more items in a series
(4) a conjunctive adverb from the rest of the sentence
(5) a nonrestrictive dependent clause
(6) conventional separations

(1) TWO SENTENCES JOINED BY A COORDINATING CONJUNCTION
(and, but, or, nor, for, so, yet)

We have already discussed how the comma comes before one of these short connectors (See Chapter Eight).
Examples:

It's is difficult to return to school when a student is older, *but* it is well worth the effort.
Harry is obsessed with pizza, *so* he eats it for breakfast.

In each of these examples, the comma is separating the first independent clause from the connector and the second independent clause.

(2) INTRODUCTORY MATERIAL FROM THE INDEPENDENT CLAUSE

Another separation marked by a comma is between material that comes before the independent clause and the independent clause itself. Because the most important parts of a sentence are the subject and verb, nearly any word, phrase, or clause that comes before these parts is separated.
Examples:

Now, you must learn to fend for yourself. (word, independent clause)
Of course, you must also learn to do your own laundry. (phrase, independent clause)
If you can take care of yourself, you will have an easier time in life. (dependent clause, independent clause)

(3) THREE OR MORE ITEMS IN A SERIES

Commas separate three or more items in a row whether the items are words, phrases, or clauses.
Examples:

Harry likes *pizza, popcorn, pretzels,* and *peanuts.* (four words in a row)
Sam looked for Hairball *under the sofa, in the cellar,* and *on the mantle.* (three phrases in a row)
Hairball likes to hide in the darnest places, he eats everything from mice to M&M's, and *he enjoys sitting on Sam's head.* (three clauses in a row)

NOTE: Occasionally, when there's no confusion between the last two items, the comma can be omitted. It may, however, be best to keep it to avoid any problem.

Florence grows *apples, oranges* and *grapes* on her forty acre farm.

(4) A CONJUNCTIVE ADVERB FROM THE REST OF THE SENTENCE

We have already seen how long connectors such as *however, therefore, consequently,* more*over, nevertheless* are followed by a comma when they are used after a semi-colon and independent clause. However, even when they are used as an adverb, they are still separated (as in this sentence). Examples:

Studying requires a commitment of time; *however,* such time may be difficult to find for the working parent.
Eating pizza for breakfast, *however,* is not good for the average person. (requires 2 commas)
Therefore, it's best to eat cereal with fruit for breakfast.
That does not mean you should go without breakfast, *however.*

(5) A NONRESTRICTIVE DEPENDENT CLAUSE

This is perhaps the most confusing use of the comma, and it is a separation requiring two commas. Take a look at this sentence:

Mary, *who is my neighbor*, wears mittens to avoid picking up any germs.
The phrase *who is my neighbor* can be considered miscellaneous information because the sentence means the same thing without it.

Mary wears mittens to avoid picking up any germs.
As a result, *who is my neighbor* takes a comma before it and a comma after it (almost like parentheses). Most often a nonrestrictive clause begins with the pronouns "who," "which," or "that."

The television, *which I bought,* broke. ("which I bought" doesn't influence the meaning)
My brother, *who is odd,* never carries pictures of his children. ("who is odd" doesn't influence the meaning)

It's up to the writer to determine what information is crucial and what isn't.
Cough syrup *that works* often eats a hole in my stomach.
Here, the clause *that works* is necessary to the meaning of the sentence and cannot be removed without changing the sense.

Movies *that are violent* should be restricted. (*that are violent* identifies *movies*)
The boy who sits in the back is my cousin. (*who sits in the back* identifies the *boy*)

(6) CONVENTIONAL SEPARATIONS

This is a broad category including many items already familiar to you:
comma between city and state (Albany, New York)
comma between day of the month and year (May 4, 1993)
comma after a salutation (Dear Sir,)

Remember: every comma you use should have a purpose, other than a pregnant pause; it should separate items to make the sentence easier to read.

LEVEL ONE EXERCISE 14.1

Insert commas wherever necessary in each of the following sentences. Some sentences may need more than one comma and others may not need any.

1. A cold capsule that works has not been invented yet.

2. Harry was born in Tucson, Arizona on May 10, 1942.

3. John, Bill and Paul went to their cabin in the Adirondack Mountains.

4. After the flood waters receded everyone pitched in to clean up the mess.

5. Money may help pay bills but it can cause too much tension in relationships.

6. The river, however, did billions of dollars worth of damage before it receded.

7. The Mississippi River which divides the United States displaced hundreds of people.

8. Of course a college degree does not guarantee that a job will be available for the graduate.

9. Larry threw his hat on the table and raced to the refrigerator for a frozen orange.

10. The haunted house had cobwebs broken windows and ripped shutters.

LEVEL TWO EXERCISE 14.1

Insert commas wherever necessary in each of the following sentences. Some sentences may need more than one comma and others may not need any.

1. John seemed rather disoriented because he had his shirt on backwards.

2. After the movie was over John Jack and Jill went out to dinner.

3. Mary's Gucci watch which was purchased in California fell apart on the plane.

4. John took Mary to the Hyatt for dinner but when the check arrived John fainted.

5. Eating junk food ,watching television and drinking Gatorade can have a negative effect on impressionable minds.

6. Harry was born in Phoenix Arizona but when he was five his family moved to Austin Texas.

7. John's daily routine consisted of feeding rats to his boa constrictor practicing Kung Fu in front of a mirror and counting his money.

8. If everyone practiced tolerance there would be less prejudice.

9. Greed however may be a part of the human condition that is too embedded to eradicate.

10. He wished upon a star and woke up a millionaire with three Mercedes and a palace in the Ozarks.

14.2 The Semi-Colon

Two basic uses for the semi-colon are to join two independent clauses and to clarify items in a series where commas are also used.

The first use was discussed in Chapter Eight.

Going to the movies used to be cheap**; now,** they are quite expensive.

The second use doesn't occur too often. Take a look at the following sentence:

Our family vacationed in Salt Lake City, Utah, Denver, Colorado, Boise, Idaho, San Diego, California and Dallas, Texas.

The commas separate the city and state, but they also separate each state and city. This sentence becomes easier to read with semi-colons between the states and cities:

Our family vacationed in Salt Lake City, Utah; Denver, Colorado; Boise, Idaho; San Diego, California; and Dallas, Texas.

Now the sentence is clearer.

LEVELS ONE AND TWO EXERCISE 14.2

Insert a semi-colon wherever necessary in each of the following. Some sentences will not require a semi-colon.

1. The current state of education is constantly being debated; however, nothing ever changes.

2. When you are in Rome, visit the Coliseum for a sense of forgotten grandeur.

3. Clearly, some dogs are spoiled by their owners; in fact, some owners are ruled by their dogs.

4. The flooding of the Mississippi River in 1993 brought people together; nevertheless, the devastation will continue to be felt for a decade.

5. The last solar eclipse was the longest in history, but many people missed it because of the cloud cover.

14.3 The Apostrophe

The apostrophe has two functions: **one is to show possession** and the **other is to show a contraction.**

(1) To show possession simply means that a noun "belongs" to someone or something. To show ownership, **'s** is added to singular nouns:

> dog's tail, child's toy, Bob's computer, Sue's dress, frame's edge

When a noun is both plural and possessive, the plural is formed first (usually by adding "s"), and the apostrophe is added to show ownership:

> dogs' tails, girls' books, cars' lights, evenings' delights

Occasionally, a plural noun is formed irregularly and requires **'s**:

> children's toys, geese's feathers

NOTE: Possessive pronouns do not require apostrophes: his, hers, its, yours, theirs.

(2) In a contraction, the apostrophe replaces the letter that is dropped to make one word:

is not = isn't	do not = don't	(' replaces the o)
it is = it's	there is = there's	(' replaces the i)
can not = can't		('replaces the n and o)

LEVEL ONE EXERCISE 14.3

Insert apostrophes wherever necessary.

1. Its about time you traded in your old car for a newer one.

2. Harrys mother is constantly nagging him to pick up his clothes.

3. Isnt it an ego boost to see your name up in lights?

4. Everyones ideas should be respected, but dont expect to agree with every idea.

5. The books binding was torn, but the pages didnt fall out.

LEVEL TWO EXERCISE 14.3

Insert apostrophes wherever necessary.

1. A nurses duties have changed over the years, though the ethics havent.

2. Harrys decision to enter the field of robotics was one of the best decisions hed ever made.

3. Some computers hardware consists of chips made by Intel, the largest manufacturer of computer microchips.

4. IBMs reorganization included hundreds of layoffs and may include many more before its reorganization is completed.

5. Lifes pleasures are often in small wonders, such as a birds flight, a flowers bloom or a whales mournful song.

14.4 The Exclamation Point

Student writers often shy away from the exclamation point needlessly. It can be used for any sentence that contains strong emotion or intense emphasis:

> The house wasn't worth a nickel!
> Homelessness is a blight on the United States!
> Eating tacos for breakfast causes serious heartburn!

Whenever you have a sentence that you feel is worth emphasizing or contains strong emotion, do use the exclamation mark. It varies the sentences, and such variety makes for more sophisticated writing and often more enjoyable reading. On the other hand, too many exclamation marks makes the reading sound hysterical!

LEVELS ONE AND TWO EXERCISE 14.4

Decide which of the following five sentences should have an exclamation point and insert it.

1. No one leaves this room until everyone has been searched.

2. As the storm approached, the golfers ran for cover.

3. Go to school or get a job.

4. Everyone is so friendly in the Bahamas.

5. Get out from under that bed — now.

14.5 The Question Mark

Most writers know that questions are indicated by a question mark. There are, however, some sentence constructions that look like questions, but are statements of fact. These sentences often include verbs like **wonder** or **think** and do not require a question mark.

> I wonder who's kissing her now. (This is a statement of fact, not a question being posed.)
> Who's kissing her now? (This is a direct question to which the writer expects a response.)

> Harry often thinks about how his ex-wife is doing. (This is a statement of fact.)
> How is Harry's ex-wife doing? (This is a direct question.)

NOTE: Remember that when you ask a question on paper, the reader responds to it silently. Questions do add variety to writing and break up long paragraphs containing declarative sentences (sentences containing fact and ending with a period).

LEVELS ONE AND TWO EXERCISE 14.5

Insert a question mark wherever necessary.

1. I often wonder about the meaning of life and my place in it.

2. Do you think the rain will come through the new roof.

3. As you age, you wonder what became of youth and agility.

4. It's how you see yourself that matters.

5. Did you hear the one about the flea in the teacup?

14.6 Miscellaneous

❏ **The Period**: Be sure that every sentence you write ends with the appropriate punctuation. If the sentence ends with a period, make sure it's clearly there, or you will have a run-on sentence.

❏ **Quotation Marks**: In Chapter Four (page 30) three ways to write the quotation are given. Just a reminder: quotation marks generally go around the actual words of the person and the end punctuation.

> "You better clean your room," Dad said, "or you're grounded."
> Dad said, "You better clean your room, or you're grounded."
> "You better clean your room, or you're grounded," Dad said.

❏ **Colon**: This piece of punctuation can often be used to introduce a list, as long as you tell the reader what the list will contain.

> Harry has several hobbies: eating, drinking, and cruising. ("hobbies" names the list)
> Harry's hobbies are as follows: eating, drinking, and cruising. ("as follows" comes before the colon)

Readers understand sentences that are correctly punctuated, and you **do** want to be certain your ideas are understood, so use punctuation carefully.

7⁰

Basic Punctuation Review Exercises

LEVEL ONE EXERCISE:

Insert the appropriate punctuation wherever necessary in each of the following.

1. The Rolling Stones are aging, but they are still popular.

2. Rap music reaches a wide audience, therefore, it has a great deal of influence.

3. Its a good idea to set educational goals before you enter college.

4. Gardening is a hobby that requires patience, persistence, and time.

5. Movie musicals arent as popular as they used to be.

6. The students homework was hastily done, consequently it received a poor grade.

7. His father said Get a job or go to school.

8. Marvin wondered about the theory of continental drift and how it affected the oceans.

9. His neighbor who had green hair had loud parties every Friday night.

10. When farmers plough their fields, sea gulls circle overhead.

11. The televisions antenna was removed after the owner signed up for cable.

12. Each professors grades are posted at the end of each semester.

13. The professors ties often clash with his suits.

√14. Did you ever consider the advantages of a two-year college.?

15. More and more people are health conscious,and they are watching their diets carefully.

16. A healthy diet consists of fruits,vegetables,and lean red meat.

√ 17. The schools administration is considering a tuition hike to pay for a new stadium.

√18. The armadillo makes a poor house pet, it is hard to train.

19. A literature course covers poetry,short stories,and dramas.

20. Grades should be less important than what is learned,but often the grades are more important.

LEVEL TWO EXERCISE

Insert the appropriate punctuation wherever necessary in each of the following.

1. Democracys greatest challenge is to accommodate the needs of a diverse population.

2. Medical technology has advanced considerably but doctors still need to be taught humility.

3. Its important to read curriculum requirements carefully otherwise you may end up taking courses that are not necessary.

4. Reading a good book listening to soothing music or watching a sunset are just a few of the many relaxation techniques available.

5. Watch out below he shouted.

6. The spotted owls fate has been debated by loggers conservation groups and government officials with conflicting results.

7. Harrys mother who is a bit eccentric often wonders why Harry looks at her strangely.

8. Shopping is considered an art form by some people consequently they practice their art as often as they can at every mall they can find.

9. The best way to sharpen your intellect is to read as much as you can this includes reading about subjects in which you may have little interest at the moment.

10. Its difficult to get everyones attention at a party but its even more difficult to get every ones attention at a concert.

11. Meditation is one way to ease stress in your life however it does require motivation location and time.

12. Hey you he shouted get off my azaleas.

13. There are several differences between a domesticated rabbit and a hare for example a hare has a much more elongated body.

14. Toy Manchester dogs look very much like miniature Dobermans but their disposition is more relaxed.

15. Native American folklore can teach us about the various tribal cultures their values and their mores.

16. Investing in stocks is risky business but investing in savings bonds is a secure way to save money however the return on bonds is less dramatic.

17. Environmentalists often suggest that what we do today will have an impact on our childrens children and beyond.

18. Robotics is a highly specialized and lucrative field however one does have to enjoy working with machinery every day.

19. The personal computer which many of us own is changing the way we think the way we entertain ourselves and the way we do business.

20. What you dream isnt as important as what dreams you make come true.

Chapter Fifteen

Glossary of Confusing Words

A glossary is a dictionary of words which belong to a specific subject or study. The following list concerns common words which student writers often misuse in a composition course.

We begin with THE BIG 5 — five sets of words which are the most troublesome for students. Be especially careful with these:

> **affect, effect**
> **its, it's**
> **their, there, they're**
> **to, too**
> **your, you're**

AFFECT, EFFECT: It is difficult to hear a pronunciation difference between these tow. Almost everyone says them the same way, causing confusion.

> AFFECT is a verb meaning to "influence" or to "put on."
> > Smoking will definitely **affect** one's health.
> > She **affected** an overly polite manner.

> EFFECT is a noun meaning "result" and in formal writing it can be a verb meaning to "bring about."
> > The **effect** of a tidal wave is devastating.
> > The election was **effected** without violence.

ITS, IT'S: These are often misused, so use caution.

> ITS is a possessive pronoun — remember that the idea of ownership must be present.
> > The car lost **its** right front wheel.
> > The government has **its** troubles.

> IT'S is a contraction (pronoun + verb) meaning "it is" or "it has."
> > **It's** going to be a long, tough winter.
> > **It's** been snowing for three dreary days.

THEIR, THERE, THEY'RE: These three are very popular in causing errors.

THEIR is a possessive pronoun — the idea of ownership must be present.
Their government is corrupt.
Where are **their** invoices?

THERE is an introductory word (an expletive) which begins many sentences. It can also mean "in that place" or "location."
There were many reasons for the Civil War.
I cannot convince him to go **there**.
Put it **there**.

THEY'RE is a contraction (pronoun + verb) meaning "they are."
The neighbors said **they're** not coming.
They're not pleased with the major's decision.

TO, TOO: These are different parts of speech that are not difficult to use correctly if you are careful.

TO is a preposition as in the phrase "to the left."
TO is found with many verbs as in "to read" or "to write."
I am going **to send** you to the principal.
To be a financial success is his dream.
Go **to** your room.

TOO has two meanings: "also" and "very" or "excessively."
She went shopping, **too**. [notice the comma]
The mall was **too** busy for me.

YOUR, YOU'RE: Since the pronunciation is the same, be careful with these.

YOUR is a possessive pronoun. Again, look for the idea of ownership.
I don't like **your** attitude.
Your directions are bewildering.

YOU'RE is a contraction for "you are."
You're not studying long enough.
He misbehaves when **you're** not here.

THE BIG 5 EXERCISES

LEVEL ONE EXERCISE:

Circle the correct word in each of the following.

1. Were you (affected, effected) by his performance?

2. Cruelty to animals always (affects, effects) me.

3. The (affects, effects) of sunlight are well known.

4. What is the (affect, effect) of mixing those two colors?

5. I think (its, it's) better to live alone.

6. (Its, It's) not easy.

7. He said (its, it's) been a profitable year.

8. The goldfish ignored (its, it's) food.

9. The students are waiting for (their, there, they're) exam.

10. When (their, there, they're) grades came, they were happy.

11. (Their, There, They're) are too many cars on the road.

12. I believe (their, there, they're) not selling tickets today.

13. That outfit is much (to, too) expensive.

14. The employees want (to, too) go right now.

15. Chili is often (to, too) hot for me to eat.

16. Sara, (to, too), is finished with her essay.

17. (Your, You're) ancestors were proud people.

18. I don't know what (your, you're) schedule is.

19. She mentioned that (your, you're) ready for a better job.

20. Hank knows what (your, you're) planning to do.

LEVEL TWO EXERCISE

Circle the correct word in each of the following.

1. My cat, Hairball, was negatively (affected, effected) when I brought a new kitten into the household.

2. One of the (affects, effects) of excessive dieting is the loss of muscle tissue.

3. Mr. Gallstone (affected, effected) great indifference to his neighbor's house fire.

4. The new accountant (affected, effected) a smooth transition to a complex computer system.

5. (Its, It's) not necessary for you to bring the matter to court.

6. I was told that (its, it's) been several years since a major snowstorm hit this area.

7. One impressive aspect of democracy is (its, it's) bloodless and civilized transfer of power.

8. The college is concerned that (its, it's) remaining open space will be filled with parking lots.

9. (Their, There, They're) will always be a promotion opportunity for a conscientious employee in this company.

10. Mr. Livermore wrote and said that (their, there, they're) not hiring until the new year.

11. The kennel found that (their, there, they're) stock of rottweilers had a bone deficiency.

12. When (their, there, they're) located near ample food supplies (their, there, they're) will always be rodents.

13. The psychiatrist tried (to, too) bring his irrational patient (to, too) his senses.

14. (To, Too) much medication can make driving quite dangerous.

15. France, (to, too), is concerned with the future of the European Community.

16. The United Nations is involved in providing food for distressed countries, (to, too).

17. If (your, you're) in the habit of smoking too much, (your, you're) in for trouble.

18. When the professor heard of (your, you're) discovery, he was elated.

19. (Your, You're) not the first, nor will you be the last, to misjudge his character.

20. I see that (your, you're) resume is carefully done, but it is too brief.

ADDITIONAL GLOSSARY ENTRIES

A, AN

We use these differently when we speak. We say **a** before a word that begins with a consonant sound, a "you" sound, or a pronounced "h." We say **an** before a vowel sound or before a silent "h."

Make the same changes when you write:

a regular guy, **a** delicious meal, **a** notebook (consonants)

a uranium mine, **a** union strike, **a** university ("you" sound)

a horror show, **a** history book, **a** heart attack (pronounced "h")

but

an application, **an** opal, **an** easy quiz (vowels)

an hour, *an* "h", **an** honor, **an** herb (silent "h")

ACCEPT, EXCEPT

ACCEPT is a verb meaning to "receive" or to "agree to."

The senator will **accept** the award himself.

The police **accepted** his alibi.

I will **accept** the terms of the loan.

EXCEPT is a verb meaning to "leave out," and it can also mean "but" or "excluding."

All "A" students were **excepted** from the final exam.

Every student is here **except** John Bright.

I am through with my finals **except** for math.

ADVICE, ADVISE

ADVICE is a noun meaning "recommendation," "suggestion," or "opinion."

My **advice** to you is to finish college.

A lawyer gives **advice** to his clients.

When I want your **advice**, I will ask.

ADVISE is a verb meaning to "make suggestions" or to "counsel."

I **advise** you to finish college.

The lawyer **advised** his clients.

When I want you to **advise** me, I will ask.

ALL RIGHT, ALRIGHT

ALL RIGHT means "acceptable," "yes," "safe" or "unharmed."

His grades are **all right** but not outstanding.

All right, you can expect my support.

I heard him fall. Is he **all right**?

ALRIGHT — avoid: this is a misspelling.

A LOT, ALOT

Student writers tend to overuse "a lot." Try to use "much," "many," or "a great deal" instead. A LOT means "several" and it is very informal and always two words.

> **A lot** of students are short of money.

> I have **a lot** to say to you.

> My cousin has **a lot** of problems at home.

ALOT — This is a misspelling — AVOID.

AMOUNT, NUMBER (see also FEWER, LESS)

AMOUNT is used when you are writing about a unit, or something you cannot count, or something taken as a whole.

> An enormous **amount of money** is needed by the schools.

> A small **amount of snow** fell on the prairie.

> The **amount of sunlight** a plant needs is variable.

NUMBER is used when you refer to individual things that can be counted.

> That auditorium has a huge **number of seats**.

> A **number of rifles** were discovered in his trunk.

> His report contained a **number of errors**.

AND ETC.

Avoid this. It is a redundancy, meaning an unnecessary repetition. "Etc." by itself means "and so forth" (et cetera).

> The old bookcase contains books, figurines, glass, **etc.**

(It is a good idea to avoid "etc." in a writing course. It asks the reader to fill in the blanks, so to speak.)

> The character in the short story was found guilty of theft, vandalism, murder, etc. [not good]

BESIDE, BESIDES

BESIDE is a preposition meaning "next to" or "by the side of."

> Stand here **beside** me.

> The file cabinet is **beside** the desk.

BESIDES is a connector (conjunctive adverb) meaning "in addition."

> He did not study while in college; **besides,** he was more interested in the military.

BUST, BUSTED

It is generally best to avoid these in a writing course because they are too informal; use "burst" or "broke" instead.

NOT: The aquarium busted wide open.

RATHER: The aquarium **burst** wide open.

NOT: I busted the computer screen.

RATHER: I **broke** the computer screen.

COULD OF, WOULD OF

These are misspellings based upon the pronunciation of "could've" and "would've." It is better to write out these contractions in your college work.

The president **could have** pardoned the traitor, but he did not.

FEWER, LESS

FEWER is used for what can be counted.

He receives **fewer TV channels** than I do.

There are **fewer trains** after midnight.

LESS is used for bulk amounts and quantities that cannot be counted.

We demand **less violence** in the movies!

Many workers today have **less leisure** time.

The students want **less homework**.

GONNA

Occasionally this slips into student writing, again because of pronunciation. Similar demons are "tuff" for "tough," "wen" for "when," "wich" for "which," and "coulda" for "could've." Take care to spell words correctly to avoid confusing the reader.

HERE'S, THERE'S, WHERE'S:

Occasionally these words create a subject/verb agreement problem. Each of these is **singular** and cannot be used with a **plural** subject, so be careful when using these contractions.

NOT: Here's several reasons for the revolution.

RATHER: **Here are** several reasons for the revolution.

NOT: There's too many politicians against it.

RATHER: **There are** too many politicians against it.

NOT: Where's the computer forms I ordered?

RATHER: **Where are** the computer forms I ordered?

      Here's the book you ordered.

      There's the culprit now.

      Where's the beef?

HISSELF

This is nonstandard English and should be avoided in formal writing.

OFF OF

This is conversational English, but in your writing, use **off** by itself.

> He was told to get **off** the stage.
>
> I am not sure how to get **off** a horse.

PASSED, PAST

> PASSED as a verb means "went by" or "handed around." Also, "passed out" means to "faint."
>
> > The fire truck **passed** me doing 60 mph.
> >
> > Professor Languid **passed** out his glossary.

> PAST as an adjective means "previous" or "former."
>
> > He made no money during the **past** year.
> >
> > Jake's **past** activities were criminal.
> >
> > The **past** president of the group moved away.

> PAST as a noun means "time gone by."
>
> > No one can change the **past**.
> >
> > The **past** is where grandmother lives.

> BE CAREFUL HERE: PAST can be an adverb, too:
>
> > The police **passed** (main verb) the intersection.
> >
> > BUT: The police went **past** the intersection. (adverb modifies verb "went")

PRINCIPLE, PRINCIPAL

> PRINCIPLE means a "rule of conduct," a "code," a "truth."
>
> > Mr. Debased lives by no **principles** at all.
> >
> > The Marines have high **principles** of behavior.
> >
> > Generosity is a valued **principle**.

> PRINCIPAL is what you want for most other meanings: "the top administrator," "chief," "main," or "first," "a loan balance."
>
> > Everybody here knows the **principal** of our high school.
> >
> > What is his **principal** reason for leaving college?
> >
> > Because the interest is high, we cannot seem to reduce our **principal**.

REASON IS BECAUSE

We hear this redundant phrase often in conversation, but it needs a slight change in formal writing. Use "the reason is that."

> **The reason** I withdrew **is that** I work forty hours a week.

> **The main reason** we are closed **is that** our computer is down.

SUPPOSE, SUPPOSED

SUPPOSE is a verb meaning to "assume" or to "believe."

> I **suppose** we have a test on Friday.

> Do you **suppose** the quiz will be difficult?

SUPPOSED can mean "should." (Do not drop the final "d" in *supposeD*, even though it is usually silent.)

> You are **supposed** to prepare your class work.

> NOT: The manager was suppose to meet us.

> RATHER: The manager was **supposed** to meet us.

THAN, THEN

THAN is a connector used in comparisons.

> India has a larger population **than** Cambodia.

> A Rolls is more expensive **than** a Lincoln.

THEN is an adverb meaning "at that time," "soon after," "next."

> There was no television **then**, to say nothing of VCR's.

> Radio was invented first, **then** television.

> The President took his oath, and **then** he gave his speech.

THEIRSELFS

This will occur once in a while if the student writer is not careful. This is nonstandard; use "themselves."

> NOT: They saw theirselfs as martyrs.

> RATHER: They saw **themselves** as martyrs.

THERE'S (see HERE'S)

THROUGH, THREW

THROUGH is a preposition which means "in one side and out the other," among many other meanings. See your dictionary. Do not confuse with THREW, which is the past form of the verb to "throw."

> Professor Baffle went **through** chapter three too quickly.

> The police searched **through** the entire school building.

Mr. Wasp **threw** us out of the movie house.

When he was **through** with the newspaper, Elmo **threw** it into the fireplace.

TOWARD, TOWARDS

Both mean the same. It is correct to use either, although some prefer the first.

USE, USED

USE is a verb which means "to utilize" or "to make use of."

I always **use** a knife to eat beans.

Use this hammer to break that window.

USED is the past form of "to use."

Professor Languid **used** one knuckle to knock on the board.

We **used** jumper cables to start the car.

NOTE: "Used" can also mean "to be accustomed to." [When you write "used" to mean this or "in the habit of," do not forget the final "d," and follow it with the word "to."]

NOT: Sasha use to take a bus to work; now she drives.

RATHER: Sasha **used to** take a bus to work; now she drives.

NOT: Alfred Hitchcock use to make extremely suspenseful movies.

RATHER: Alfred Hitchcock **used to** make extremely suspenseful movies.

WEATHER, WHETHER

WEATHER refers to the atmosphere and what's happening there.

Hairball, my cat, dislikes rainy **weather**.

Regardless of the **weather**, Auntie Upp is in her garden every day.

WHETHER is a conjunction used to suggest one of two possibilities. Remember that unless you are talking about the climate, use "whether."

Professor Wordy keeps talking **whether** anyone is listening or not.

Whether you graduate or not is entirely up to you.

[Sometimes "whether" is used instead of "if."]

I do not know **whether** Senator Stalwart left town.

WERE, WE'RE

WERE is the past form of the verb "are."

Ms. Placid and Professor Blur **were** at a boring party last night.

Where **were** they when the hurricane struck?

WE'RE is the contraction [pronoun + verb] of "we are."

I bet **we're** going to be tested on the glossary.

We're certain Sebastion said he came from France.

WHERE'S (see HERE'S)

WHOSE, WHO'S

WHOSE is a possessive pronoun and indicates ownership.

Alexander the Great, **whose** soldiers loved him, wanted nothing but more and more territory.

Whose diamond and emerald necklace is this?

WHO'S is a contraction for either "who is" or "who has" [pronoun + verb].

Who's seen the movie *Gone With the Wind*?

Professor Ample is looking for the person **who's** responsible for the saucy drawing on the blackboard.

 **Don't forget to look up unfamiliar words!**

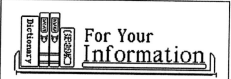

For Your Information

To help increase your vocabulary, use a thesaurus to find new words that add zip to your writing.

LEVEL ONE EXERCISE:

Circle the correct word.

1. I refuse to bring him (a, **an**) apple.

2. If he gives you a "D," (**accept**, except) it gracefully.

3. Joanna said goodbye to everyone (accept, **except**) me.

4. He can cause (**a lot**, alot) of trouble when he wants to.

5. Saavas refused to sit (**beside**, besides) Sebastion.

6. (**Here's**, Here are) several bananas for you.

7. Auntie Upp (**could've**, could of) hit the ceiling.

8. He rushed (**passed**, past) us like a maniac on fire.

9. I told Marko to stop talking to (hisself, **himself**).

10. Sam (busted, **broke**) his food processor.

11. Let me tell you what I'm (**gonna**, going to) do.

12. Jones (**use**, used) to see a movie every Saturday.

13. The reason I came back to college is (**because**, that) I am tired of making minimum wage.

14. Everyone knows Mr. Debased has no (principals, **principles**) and cannot be trusted.

15. Mr. Impulse suddenly (through, **threw**) his keys out the window.

16. Professor Languid was driving (**toward**, towards) the college when his car blew up.

17. (Were, **We're**) not sure if he got to work on time.

18. Sun Lee doesn't care (weather, **whether**) he sees Korea again or not.

19. (Where's, **Where are**) the tires I bought for the car?

20. They only have (theirselves, **themselves**) to blame.

LEVEL TWO EXERCISE: *80*

Circle the correct word in each of the following.

1. If you are lucky enough to become an octogenarian, you probably will have some wise (advise, advice) to pass along on growing old successfully.

2. Hairball, my cat, fell, jumped, or was pushed out of a third floor window; fortunately, he is (all right, alright).

3. Today (fewer, less) college students are able to pay all of the bills for four years of bar hopping.

4. (There's, There are) several reasons why you should encourage your children to leave home as often as possible.

5. The tuba player almost made it (passed, past) the dignitaries' platform when he fell on his bell.

6. The Quibblers' Society didn't know (weather, whether) to sue for damages or not.

✓ 7. Senator Stalwart's (principal, principle) objection to the Civil Liberties Union was that it never relaxed.

✓ 8. The reason Mr. Faulty found himself in jail is (that, because) he called Judge Fossil a jerk.

9. Joe Clown was usually quite proud of (hisself, himself) even when he passed out on booze.

10. (Whose, Who's) responsible for hiding the team's track shoes?

11. Professor Cash has seen more of the world's luxury resorts (than, then) any other faculty member.

12. Professor Cloudy was delighted that on Saturday he was to (accept, except) the Weatherman-of-the-Year Award.

✓ 13. A small (number, amount) of kindergarten children ran out on stage and sang "Itsy Bitsy Spider" — twice.

14. "(Through, Threw) thick and thin," "come hell or high water," "for better or for worse," and "in this great moment of need" are all cliches and should be avoided.

15. (Beside, Besides) being a professional movie maker, Alfred Hitchcock was considered to be a great wit.

√ 16. Mr. Gallstone (busted, broke) through the doors of the Bovine Society's meeting room and threw a glass of milk at Mrs. Counterpane. She retaliated by hitting him in the face with a whipped cream pie.

17. Officer Whistle lurched out of his police car and demanded to know (weather, whether) we had permission to be on the street after 11 p.m.

18. (There's, There are) one very monotonous thing about Greece, according to Saavas, and that is the constant sunshine.

19. Having ducks on the family pond is (alright, all right) with me, but Grandfather Casanova doesn't like their toilet habits.

20. Sam and his wife will be the (principle, principal) guests at the chicken wings and beef-on-weck banquet.

Index

A

B

C

Q

R